Research Paper Procedure

HIGH SCHOOL

SECOND EDITION

by Amy M. Kleppner

Illustrations by Caroline A. James

TEACHER'S
Discovery®
©2007

Published by:
Teacher's Discovery®
2676 Paldan Drive
Auburn Hills, MI 48326
www.teachersdiscovery.com

To order English/language arts materials:
Teacher's Discovery® English Division   Phone: 1-800-583-6454
2676 Paldan Drive, Suite A   Fax: 1-888-395-6686
Auburn Hills, MI 48326

To order social studies materials:
Teacher's Discovery® Social Studies Division   Phone: 1-800-543-4180
2676 Paldan Drive, Suite B   Fax: 1-888-395-1492
Auburn Hills, MI 48326

To order science materials:
Teacher's Discovery® Science Division   Phone: 1-888-977-2436
2676 Paldan Drive, Suite C   Fax: 1-888-987-2436
Auburn Hills, MI 48326

To order Spanish, French and German language materials:
Teacher's Discovery® Foreign Language Division   Phone: 1-800-832-2437
2741 Paldan Drive   Fax: 1-800-287-4509
Auburn Hills, MI 48326

ISBN: 0-7560-0331-8
SKU: TB863E/TS2041

Introduction

During your four years in high school, you will have the opportunity to do research in many fields. You may want to give an informative speech in an English class, perhaps on the evolution of football, or maybe on the psychology of roller coaster construction. Your biology teacher may assign a debate on an issue in bioethics, for example, to present the arguments for or against doctor-assisted suicide. You may decide to write a paper showing how Jack London used his own adventurous life in writing his fiction; to present a dramatic monologue by an American sailor captured by the British during the War of 1812; or to provide the commentary for a slide show on action-in-repose in Michelangelo's slave sculptures. Or perhaps you're considering a PowerPoint presentation on the dangers of using the drug Ecstasy.

The purpose of this manual is to provide guidelines to help you complete these projects successfully. Your research will take you first to your school's media center, and that will link you to an amazing variety of sources beyond the books, magazines, newspapers, pamphlets, reprints of articles, and other material available there. Research today is a global endeavor, and you are likely to uncover much more information than you can possibly use. And that is only the beginning: beyond the electronic links to county and university libraries, to databases covering every conceivable subject, and to CD-ROMs and Web sites, there are dozens of other information sources, including interviews, surveys, family histories, videos, films, and recordings.

You will discover the many pleasures of doing research: the excitement of discovering new material; the fun of working independently; the satisfaction of producing a well-organized paper from a chaos of note cards, printouts, outlines, and preliminary drafts. And you'll acquire skills that will serve you throughout your life. As a professional, you may conduct research in science, medicine, law, social science, or the humanities. On a personal level, you may want to trace your family's roots through genealogical research. As a community activist, you may need to study your city's budget for education or the area's transportation needs.

Welcome to the world of scholarship, research, and intellectual growth.

Acknowledgments

It is a pleasure to acknowledge those who contributed valuable help to the creation of this manual. Ginny Trulio and the media center staff at Walt Whitman High School in Bethesda, Maryland, provided inspiration, encouragement, and information ("When was the first women's college basketball game played?") throughout the long process of composition, revision, and publication.

Several members of the English and Social Studies Departments at Whitman read earlier drafts, provided student work, and offered helpful suggestions. Lisa Baker, Penny Mayorga, and Jo Tunstall helped in ways too numerous to mention. Marjorie Geldon, Media Specialist at Newport Mill Middle School, Kensington, Maryland, kindly gave permission to use the Web Site Evaluation Form that you'll find in Appendix D, and the helpful tables in Appendix E.

Dr. Jerome Marco, principal at Walt Whitman High School, deserves special thanks for supporting the effort to develop <u>Research Paper Procedure</u>. His enthusiasm and help were crucial in starting and continuing the process that led to its publication.

I want to thank my husband, Adam Kleppner, for technical help, and my sons Bram and Caleb, for invaluable editorial comments ("Hokey!" "You've got to be kidding!").

Several recent Whitman graduates also made valuable contributions: Caroline James's fine drawings, and the model research papers by Portia Cornell, Jason Rosensweig, and Simon Chin are welcome additions to the manual.

I am also grateful to Witt J. Farquhar, a teacher in the Humanities Department at the Maret School in Washington, DC, who provided a model research paper by a science student, something the first edition of the book lacked. Appendix C now includes an excellent paper by Jeffrey Dickinson, who participated in the Maret School's Subtropical Zone Ecology Program (Sanibel Island/Vaca Key, Florida).

Finally, Margaret Marple is most deserving of thanks for providing the layout and design of this book. Her expertise has greatly improved its appearance and readability, and I am extremely grateful to her for turning an ugly duckling into a swan.

I also wish to thank in advance all those who send me comments, criticism, suggestions, and the like to improve future editions of this manual: akleppner@surfglobal.net

Amy M. Kleppner

Contents

Introduction iii

Acknowledgments iv

Contents v

Chapter 1—Overview of the Research Process 1

Chapter 2—Plagiarism, and How to Avoid It 7

Examples of Celebrity Plagiarism 7
Avoiding Plagiarism—Five Simple Rules 8

Chapter 3—Resources 15

School Media Center 15
Other Libraries 20
The World Wide Web on the Internet 21
        Tips for Searching the Internet 21

Chapter 4—Topic Selection 27

Chapter 5—Narrowing the Topic 31

Chapter 6—Formulating a Thesis Statement 35

Chapter 7—Supporting a Thesis Statement 39

Chapter 8—Creating a Topic Outline 45

Chapter 9A—Source Cards MLA 50

Sample Source Cards–MLA 50

Chapter 9B—Source Cards APA 56

Sample Source Cards–APA 60

Chapter 10—Targeting Useful Information 61

Review 61
Future Steps 63
Getting Stupid 65
Getting Stupid–Annotated 72

Chapter 11—Using Relevant Material 79

Chapter 12—Taking Notes 84

Steps in Note Taking 85

Contents

Sample Note Cards 88

Chapter 13—From Notes to Rough Draft 91

Chapter 14—Paraphrasing and Summarizing 101

Paraphrasing.. 101
Summarizing 103

Chapter 15—Using Direct Quotation 107

General Rules... 107
Lead-Ins for Quotations 110
Lead-Ins from a Professional Writer 112
Providing Follow-Ups of Direct Quotations 113

Chapter 16A—Parenthetical Documentation MLA 119

Chapter 16B—Parenthetical Documentation APA......................... 125

Chapter 17—Using Titles Correctly 131

Chapter 18—The Introduction and Conclusion 135

Introduction.. 135
Conclusion 138

Chapter 19—Revising and Proofreading 143

Checklist for Revising and Proofreading Your Research Paper 146
Proofreading and Correction Symbols 149

Chapter 20A—Works Cited—MLA 153

Periodicals 158
Other Sources 159
Electronic Sources 160
CD-ROM Programs 164
Other Electronic Sources 165

Chapter 20B—References—APA 169

Periodicals 172
Books, Brochures, and Book Chapters 173
Audiovisual Media.. 175
Electronic Sources 176
CD-ROM Programs 179
Other Electronic Sources 180

Appendix A—Outlines for Research Papers...................................... 183

Revised Topic Outline for a Research Paper 183
Position Paper Outline 184

Appendix B—Primary and Secondary Sources 185

Appendix C—Model Research Papers 187

Portia Cornell, Surviving Adolescence with Magic.. 188
Jason Rosensweig, The Holy Grail: More than a Christian Cup 196
Simon Chin, Censorship of As I Lay Dying: Yoknapatawpha in Peril...................... 203
Jeffrey Dickinson, The Osprey: An Overview and Sanibel Snapshot........................ 211

Appendix D—Using the Internet **219**

    Search Tool Terminology 219

    Search Engines 220

    Meta-Search Tools 222

    Subject Directories 224

    Starting Points 225

    Libraries 227

    Information Sources for Specific Disciplines 228

        Literature, Arts, and Humanities 228

        Science 229

        Social Science 229

    Evaluating Web Sites 230

    Web Site Evaluation Form 231

Appendix E—Citations at a Glance **233**

    MLA—Print Resources 233

    MLA—Online Resources 234

    APA—Print Resources 235

    APA—Online Resources 236

Chapter 1
Overview of the Research Process

This chapter provides an overview of the whole research process; it maps the journey you are about to make. It shows the many steps you will have to take between starting point and destination, and it reminds you that doing an excellent job will require a good deal of time and effort. The chapters that follow provide a detailed description of each step, along with suggestions for avoiding roadblocks and breakdowns.

Step 1.   **Locate, within a general subject area, a topic that fascinates you**.

Example: Acid rain

See: Chapter 4   Topic Selection

Step 2.   **Narrow the topic** by finding a specific angle or approach to it so that you can handle it within the prescribed page limit.

Example: The effect of acid rain on northeastern forests

See: Chapter 5   Narrowing the Topic

Step 3.   In the Media Center, **search for sources** of information and record publication information about books, magazines, Web sites, etc., on your 3x5 source cards, following exactly either MLA or APA form, depending on your teacher's instructions.

See: Chapter 3   Resources

                Chapters 9A   Source Cards
                    or 9B

                Pg. 50 (MLA)   Sample source cards

                Pg. 56 (APA)   Sample source cards

Step 4.   **Formulate a thesis statement** (Th S) and a clear method of development (MOD). Your thesis statement usually contains a judgment, evaluation, or criticism; it states the main idea of your paper. Your MOD shows how you are going to support your thesis.

Example: Acid rain harms forests by damaging leaves, limiting nutrients, and poisoning with toxic substances.

See: Chapter 6   Formulating a Thesis Statement

Step 5.   **Make a tentative Topic Outline**, writing your thesis statement at the top and indicating the major topics that support it. Under each topic, leave space for listing facts, examples, and supporting details that your research will provide.

See: Chapter 7   Finding Supporting Topics

Chapter 8   Creating a Topic Outline

Appendix A   Topic Outlines

Step 6.   Take your second set of index cards (4x6 or larger), called note cards, and write a **Topic Heading** on the first few cards; these are the Major Topics from your Topic Outline.

Example: Card 1. Leaf Damage

Card 2. Nutrient Limitation

Card 3. Poisoning

See: Chapter 10   Targeting Useful Information

Chapter 11   Using Relevant Material

Step 7.   **Locate sources and begin taking notes**, selecting only relevant information and entering it only under the appropriate topic headings on your note cards. Use a separate card for each idea or piece of information.

See: Chapter 10   Targeting Useful Information

Chapter 11   Using Relevant Material

Chapter 12   Taking Notes

Pg. 88   Sample note card

Step 8.   Once you have sufficient information, **organize your note cards under your major topics and return to your topic outline**. Now fill in the subtopics under your major topics. These are the facts, examples, statistics, and expert opinions that support each major topic.

Example: A.   Nutrient Limitation (major topic)

1.   Atmospheric nitrogen deposited on a forested watershed in Maine (Specific support 1)

2.   Support 2

3.   Support 3

B.   Poisoning (major topic)

1.   Red spruce decline near Bay of Fundy (Support 1)

See: Chapter 8   Creating a Topic Outline

Appendix A   Topic Outlines

Step 9.   With your completed outline and the information on your note cards in hand, start **writing your rough draft**, putting in documentation for all borrowed material as you write. Use paraphrasing, summarizing, and direct quotation, as appropriate, and provide discussion of borrowed material.

See: Chapter 13   From Notes to Rough Draft

Chapter 14   Paraphrasing and Summarizing

Chapter 15   Using Direct Quotation

Chapter 16A   Parenthetical Documentation—MLA

Chapter 16B   Parenthetical Documentation—APA

Chapter 18   Introduction and Conclusion

Step 10.   **Self-edit; exchange your paper with other students**; study the feedback you receive from peers and teachers; then **revise, revise**, and **revise**. Use a checklist.

See: Chapter 19   Revising and Proofreading

Chapter 17   Using Titles Correctly

Step 11.   When your rough draft is the best you can make it, **prepare your final version, including a works cited or references page** at the end, based on the source cards you used. Run a spelling checker, make corrections, and proofread carefully. If instructed to do so, provide a title page, or attach the cover sheet that your teacher gave you.

See: Chapter 20A   Works Cited—MLA

          Chapter 20B   References—APA

Step 12.   **Submit your paper on time and with pride,** knowing that it is your best work.

Note:

As the Contents page indicates, this manual provides two forms for the documentation of research papers: the first is the form the Modern Language Association (MLA) recommends*; the second is the form the American Psychological Association (APA) recommends.**

The MLA is an organization of teachers and scholars, founded in 1883, to strengthen teaching in languages and literature. It developed the <u>MLA Handbook</u> to simplify the task of preparing both student papers and scholarly works. The majority of scholarly publications in languages and literature follow MLA guidelines, as do many schools and colleges.

The APA, also an organization of teachers and scholars, promotes research and scholarship in psychology. Its <u>Publication Manual</u> is a widely recognized authority for publications in the social sciences. To accommodate the science and social studies departments in many schools, this manual provides APA rules and models as well.

There are other authorities on these matters, and when you are in college, <u>The Chicago Manual of Style</u> or a manual prepared by the college or university may be your guide.

Regardless of the method they advocate, the goal of all style manuals is the same: to make it easier to convey information with consistency, clarity, accuracy, and honesty.

---

* Joseph Gibaldi, MLA <u>Handbook for Writers of Research Papers</u>, 6th ed. (New York: Modern Language Association, 2003). See also Frequently Asked Questions at the MLA Web site. Updated 9 Sep. 2003. 8 Apr. 2004 <http://www.mla.org/style_faq>.

** American Psychological Association, Publication Manual of the American Psychological Association, 6th ed. (Washington, DC: APA, 2001). See also the APA <u>Publication Manual</u> Web site. 27 Feb. 2004 <http://www.apastyle.org/elecref.html>. Information about documentation for electronic sources is available in a separate publication: APA, <u>APA Style Guide for Electronic References</u>, downloadable in PDF format. This work contains the same information as the <u>Publication Manual</u>.

Chapter 2
Plagiarism, and How to Avoid It

According to the <u>American Heritage Dictionary of the English Language</u>, to plagiarize means "to steal and use (the writings of another) as one's own."

> **Note:**
>
> Even when it is unintentional, presenting someone else's thoughts, ideas, expressions, or information without proper acknowledgment of the source is an act of academic dishonesty.

This chapter provides a detailed account of the rules that will help you avoid plagiarism.

Examples of Celebrity Plagiarism

After years of being primarily a dirty secret in the academic world, plagiarism has recently been making headlines.

- Authors of best sellers, Alex Haley (<u>Roots</u>) and Gail Sheehy (<u>Passages</u>), faced lawsuits for failing to document passages apparently lifted from other books.

- Well-known historians Stephen Ambrose and Doris Kearns Goodwin had to answer the charge that several paragraphs in their best-selling books bore a close resemblance to those of other authors. The famous writers blamed sloppy scholarship and careless note-taking.

- Brian VanDeMark's publisher withdrew copies of his book, <u>Pandora's Keepers: Nine Men and the Atomic Bomb</u>, after four historians charged that he copied from their work; he promised to improve his paraphrasing and attribution.

The consequences in these cases included loss of reputation, resignations, public apologies, and substantial out-of-court settlements.

Nor is plagiarism only a writer's problem. It has done in politicians as well.

- Senator Joseph Biden's presidential bid crashed in 1987 when a reporter observed an uncanny similarity between passages in a Biden speech and those in a speech by Neil Kinnoch, a British Labour Party leader.

Recently the University of Virginia responded to plagiarism and cheating scandals with expulsions and even with the revocation of previously awarded degrees. Other colleges and many high schools have started using software programs, such as those from Canexus.com and Turnitin.com, not only to catch plagiarizers but more important, to teach students how to avoid the problem. And suspicious teachers have learned to look first at popular Web sites like geniuspapers, Research Associates, Sparknotes, and PinkMonkey.

The penalties for plagiarism vary from school to school. They often include:

- Receiving a zero for the assignment
- Doing an alternative assignment but without the possibility of improving the grade
- Parental notification
- Suspension

Teachers point out that the college recommendations they complete usually require a statement about the student's integrity.

It is not difficult to avoid plagiarism and its penalties. The instructors at the Baltimore County Learning Center of the University of Maryland have formulated some rules that are enormously helpful, and Janet Graham has given us permission to distribute them, with modifications.

> **Note**:
>
> Remember that in a research paper, your teacher will assume that any idea not cited is your own. Whenever you use other people's ideas or words, you must give them credit, whether the source is print or electronic.

Avoiding Plagiarism—Five Simple Rules

Rule 1.   A fact that is not common knowledge must have a citation.

> Scientists have found that the featherless chicken makes as much protein as the feathered chicken ("Featherless" 43).

You may write a fact that is common knowledge—something that most people in the society would know—without a citation. For example, you need not cite statements like "The United States desired independence from Great Britain in 1776." Familiar proverbs and sayings such as "Haste makes waste" also do not require citations.

Rule 2.　When you write about an idea, you must make clear whose idea it is. If it is your own idea, you do not cite the source.

> After reading several of Fitzgerald's short stories, one can see that Fitzgerald frequently takes the position of the outsider.

No citation– student's own observation

> The tone and structure of the poem suggest peace and repose.

No citation– student's own observation

Rule 3.　If you are writing about someone else's idea, you must cite your source.

> By the year 1856, San Francisco's growth was practically certain (Lotchkin 60).

> One might compare Kobe Bryant's downfall to that of Macbeth (Obel-Omia

Rule 4.　If you use someone else's exact words, you must put them in quotation marks and cite the source.

> Later, the author wrote, "Chapter VII (the hotel scene) will never be quite up to mark–I've worried about it too long and I can't quite place Daisy's reaction" (Fitzgerald 9).

Rule 5.　When you use an author's idea without quoting exactly, you must write the idea in your own words, not just rearrange or change a few of his or her words, and you must cite the source.

Original:

"White" ball, then, is the basketball of patience, method and sometimes brute strength. "Black" ball is the basketball of electric self-expression. One player has all the time in the world to perfect his skills, the other a need to prove himself. These are slippery categories, because a poor boy who is black can play "white" and a white boy of middle-class parents can play "black" (Greenfield 215).

Unacceptable paraphrase:

> "White" ball is playing basketball in a patient, methodical, strong way. "Black" ball is the game of electric self-expression. The white player takes his time to perfect his skills, but the black player wants to prove himself. These categories, however, are slippery. A poor black may play "white," and a middle-class white boy may play "black."

This follows the writer's words so closely that it is definitely plagiarism. The student did not use his or her own words to state the idea, nor is the source cited. Both paraphrasing and citation are required.

Acceptable paraphrase:

> According to Jeff Greenfield, there are fundamental differences between the "white" and the "black" style of basketball. The white player is less hurried; he takes his time, practices his skills systematically, and develops his strength. The black player, on the other hand, proves himself by playing with an almost theatrical flair. Of course, there are exceptions to these categories (215).

The student restates the writer's idea in the student's own words and cites the source of the idea. Note that when the author's name–Jeff Greenfield–occurs in the text, the student does not repeat it in the citation but gives only the page.

Use a direct quotation only when the writer has expressed his or her ideas so perfectly that you could not do them justice with a paraphrase. In that case, use Rule 4. Otherwise, summarize the main point in your own words, following Rule 5.

To help you avoid this, the most common form of plagiarism, here is a summary of the important points to keep in mind:

On your note cards:

- Take careful, **word-for-word** notes.
- Be scrupulous about the accuracy of wording, punctuation, capitalization, and sources.
- Don't try to paraphrase as you take down information; record it exactly. Paraphrase and summarize later when you draft your paper.

- When you want to add comments and observations of your own, distinguish them clearly from copied material. Use ink of a different color, or enclose your own ideas in brackets. Or add another card, with the same heading and with yourself as author.

In your rough draft:

- Cite as you write. Put in citations for all borrowed material **as you write your first draft**. Never leave this until later, thinking you will insert sources another time. Trying to find sources later for every citation is tedious.

- Remember that you must acknowledge all borrowed material, **whether you use a direct quote, a paraphrase, or a summary**. You must express information and ideas entirely in your own words, provide a parenthetical citation in the text, and list the source on your works cited or references page, formerly known as the bibliography.

- Always go the note card route. Copying material directly into your paper is one of the surest ways to plagiarize. And downloading Internet documents into your paper is a shortcut to disaster.

In your final version:

- Check your entire paper carefully to make sure that you have included all required parenthetical citations, that they are accurate, and that you have punctuated them correctly.

- Check your works cited or references page for form and accuracy, making sure that your in-text citations correspond to your list of works cited. For example, if (Denby 75) appears in your paper, then your works cited page must include the following entry: Denby, David. <u>American Sucker</u>. New York: Little, 2004.

Three more varieties of plagiarism that you must avoid:

1. **Self-plagiarism**—Submitting a paper that you submitted in a previous class.

   If you contemplate reworking a paper that you've turned in anytime in the past, check with your teacher. In general, self-plagiarism is not acceptable. Don't be like Donald, who wrote a personal narrative about winning the cakewalk in fifth grade and then submitted variations of the same essay every year until he graduated from high school.

2. **Purchasing a research paper from any source**, or copying part or all of another student's paper

   A student who offers to share papers, journal entries, homework assignments, and the like does you a great disservice. These are acts of academic dishonesty and are likely to incur penalties for both parties. Buying a paper may cost you a lot more than $20 a page—it may cost you your integrity and your reputation.

3. **Collaborative efforts** except where the teacher explicitly permits and encourages cooperation

   Unless the instructions for a project specifically allow group work, then the teacher assumes that what you submit is your work alone and is not the result of collaboration with others. When in doubt, check with your teacher.

Because plagiarism has become an increasingly serious problem as students use more and more Internet sources in their research papers, the Modern Language Association has added a greatly expanded chapter on the subject in the sixth edition of the <u>MLA Handbook</u>, cited in Chapter 1. This chapter is worth a careful reading.*

Summary

Rules about Plagiarism

- Well-known facts require no citation.

- Your own ideas require no citation.

- You must cite the source of someone else's ideas, facts, and opinions.

- Using someone else's exact words requires quotation marks and citation of the source.

- Using an author's idea but not quoting it exactly requires a thorough paraphrase, not just a rearrangement of words, and citation of the source.

---

*A highly entertaining and informative book on this subject is Thomas Mallon, <u>Stolen Words: The Classic Book on Plagiarism</u> (New York: Harcourt, 1989).

Chapter 3
Resources

This chapter discusses three of the most valuable sources of information available to help you with your research: 1. the school media center; 2. public and university libraries; 3. the Internet. Because school media centers and public libraries are organized in many different ways, this will be only a brief tour. It's a good idea to familiarize yourself with the libraries in your area and with the helpful people who staff them.

1.   School Media Center

For several reasons, this is the place to start. The media center at your own school probably has material that librarians have selected specifically to facilitate students' research projects. Furthermore, tapping into the media center's specialized databases first to narrow your search is more efficient than just punching in key words for an Internet search engine. And looking into books, magazines, reference works, and the like in the media center can uncover much useful information. Surprisingly enough, there is a lot of valuable material that you won't find on the Internet.

First, there are **print resources**—books, magazines, newspapers, and newsletters. These may include hard copy, microfiche, and microfilm. There are reference works like World Book, The Encyclopedia of the Middle Ages, or Guide to the Supreme Court. These are often the best place to find background information, even though your research will take you far beyond encyclopedias, almanacs, and atlases. Most media centers now use electronic catalogs, which often provide access to other library catalogs.

Second, there are **nonprint resources**—videos, films, filmstrips, records, audiotapes, slides, photographs, and art works. These are also usually listed in the electronic catalog.

Third, there are **electronic resources**—computer programs, CD-ROMs, subscription databases on the Internet, and Internet Web sites. Many schools provide students with Internet accounts so they can search worldwide for needed information. Often students can access subscription databases both from the school media center and from home by using a password. We will describe a few of these databases in more detail below.

Fourth, there are **human resources**—the media center staff, who are knowledgeable and are eager to help you do your best.

Information Databases on the Internet

In addition to the magazines stored in the workroom, many school media centers and public libraries subscribe to electronic databases that make hundreds of articles in periodicals immediately available. Starting your electronic search with these databases, where some prior selection has reduced the volume, will be a huge time saver. These sites are normally password-protected; they are available through subscription to schools and libraries. Some include citation information. A few of the most popular databases in school media centers are the following.

Table 1

Online Periodical Services—Subscription-based	
Source	**Description**
CQ Researcher (Congressional Quarterly) http://www.library.cqpress.com/ cqresearcher	An excellent source for information about political and social issues, including topics in health, international affairs, education, environment, technology, and the U.S. economy. Includes citation information and help with topic selection.
EBSCOhost http://www.epnet.com	A collection of single databases, including MasterFile Premier (general interest), Health Source, Newspaper Source, EBSCO Animals, and ERIC (Educational Resource Information Center). There are also databases covering other subject areas and some designed specifically for elementary and middle school students.
HighBeam Research http://www.highbeam.com/library	An online periodical database with index and full text of magazine and newspaper articles. It has over 32 million documents from 2,800 sources, including books, magazines, newspapers, maps, pictures, and radio and TV transcripts. It includes reference works and academic and scientific journals.
Facts.com http://www.facts.com	A source of news items covering historic events, key issues, statistics, and people from the last 60+ years. Includes biographies, obituaries, editorials, historic documents, country profiles, indexes, maps, photos, and graphics. Its databases include World News Digest, Facts on File, World News Special Features, Reuters News, Issues and Controversies, and Today's Science.
InfoTrac http://infotrac.galegroup.com/ itweb	A collection of databases covering general interest topics, business, arts, humanities and social sciences, technology, and health. There are collections specifically for elementary, middle school, and high school students. Included are full-text articles and pictures from newspapers, periodicals, reference books, and scholarly journals. InfoTrac Onefile, General Reference Center Gold, and Expanded Academic ASAP are general subject databases.
Newsbank http://www.newsbank.com	Provides information from hundreds of newspapers. There are four databases: American Newspapers, with full-text articles from 500 newspapers; Special Reports, focusing on Postwar Iraq, War on Terrorism, Infectious Diseases, Mental Health, Black History, and Environment; African-American Experience, including images, biographies, debates, documents, and slave narratives; and the Chicago Tribune historical archive, covering the events and issues of the past 150 years on topics ranging from architecture to Chicago gangsters to the Vietnam War.

Online Periodical Services—Subscription-based

Source	Description
Polling the Nations http://poll.orspub.com	A survey database covering over 5000 topics, ranging from Abortion, Affirmative Action, and AIDS to Zaire, Zimbabwe, and Zoos. It contains over 500,000 questions from 14,000 surveys, conducted in the U.S. and over 100 other countries from 1986 to the present.
Pro and Con Online http://pro-and-con.org	Provides articles from three publications: <u>Congressional Digest</u>, covering controversial issues before Congress; <u>Supreme Court Debates</u>, analysis of cases before the U.S. Supreme Court; and <u>International Debates</u>, on current issues before the United Nations and other international forums. Articles from this database date from 1998 to the present.
ProQuest http://proquest.umi.com/login	A computerized index with abstracts or full text of articles from hundreds of periodicals, scholarly journals, and newspapers since 1986. It includes ProQuest Platinum, Research Library, Newsstand, and Historical Newspapers, containing full-text articles from the <u>New York Times</u>, <u>Washington Post</u>, <u>Wall Street Journal</u>, and <u>Christian Science Monitor</u>.
SIRS Knowledge Source (Social Issues Resources Series) http://sks.sirs.com	Provides integrated online access to full-text articles and Internet resources from SIRS reference databases including SIRS Researcher, SIRS Government Reporter, SIRS Renaissance, and SKS WebSelect. Has citation information. **SIRS Discoverer**—A general reference database designed for young researchers. Provides information on a wide range of topics, including animals, drugs and alcohol, environment, history and government, science, social issues, sports, and technology. Includes current events, reference works, maps, and pictures. **SIRS Government Reporter**—A valuable source for historic and government documents, directories, and almanacs. Includes country profiles, information about federal agencies, Congress and Presidents, National Archive documents, and U.S. Supreme Court decisions. **SIRS Renaissance**—Provides current perspectives on the arts and humanities, including architecture, culture, literature, multimedia, music, performing arts, philosophy and religion, and visual arts. Includes art reproductions, photographs, illustrations, and maps. **SIRS Researcher**—An index and full-text articles on general reference, including social issues, health, science, business, and global issues from 1988 to the present from hundreds of domestic and international magazines, newspapers, and governmental publications. **SKS WebSelect**—Provides information on general reference topics, including astronomy and space, HIV/AIDS, infectious diseases, substance abuse, and terrorism.

In addition to the databases discussed above, a number of important reference works are now accessible online in many school and public libraries. Find out if your media center subscribes to any of the books listed below. Bear in mind that in many cases, if the online version is not available, there may be a CD-ROM or a print version.

Table 2

Online Encyclopedias and Other Books—Subscription-Based	
Source	**Description**
American National Biography Online http://www.anb.org	This powerful database provides biographical information about 17,400 men and women (deceased only), who influenced American history. It is updated four times a year and includes illustrations, cross-references, and links to selected Web sites.
Columbia Granger's World of Poetry Online http://www.columbiagrangers.org	Included in the online edition are the following: <u>The Classic Hundred Poems</u>; <u>Top 500 Poems</u>; <u>Index to Poetry in Anthologies</u>; <u>Index to Poetry in Collected and Selected Works</u>; and <u>Index to African-American Poetry</u>. A number of Granger's reference works are available in print, CD-ROM, and online versions.
Encyclopedia Britannica Online http://www.eb.com	The full text of the <u>Encyclopedia Britannica</u> is available free of charge on the Internet at www.britannica.com. The subscription service for either Premium Service or School Edition provides additional features.
Grolier Multimedia Encyclopedia http://go.grolier.com	The whole package includes <u>Encyclopedia Americana</u>, <u>Grolier Multimedia Encyclopedia</u>, <u>New Book of Knowledge</u>, <u>Nueva enciclopedia cumbre</u>, <u>New Book of Popular Science</u>, <u>Lands and Peoples</u>, and <u>America the Beautiful</u>, plus five dictionaries, two thesauri, and an interactive atlas. Many libraries may subscribe to only one or two of these books.
Information Please Almanac http://www.infoplease.com	Provides information under the following categories: world, U.S., history and government, biography, sports, arts and entertainment, business, society and culture, and health and science. Information sources include almanacs, atlas, dictionary, and encyclopedia.
Oxford English Dictionary Online http://dictionary.oed.com	The <u>OED</u> is available in three versions: print, CD-ROM, and online.
World Book Encyclopedia Online http://www.worldbookonline.com	Provides full-text articles from the 22-volume set and from books and documents in major subject areas. Additional reference works include the <u>World Book Spanish-Language Encyclopedia</u>.

Table 3

Online Content Services—Subscription-Based	
Source	**Description**
Background Notes http://www.state.gov/r/pa/ei/bgn	Information from the Department of State on the approximately 200 countries with which the U.S. has relations. Includes facts about land, people, history, government, political conditions, and economy. Online access is free; print versions are sold by subscription.
The Economist http://www.economist.com	An independent source for global economic and political news and analysis. Includes research tools and data bank.

Online Content Services—Subscription-Based

Source	Description
Gale Databases http://infotrac.galegroup.com	In addition to print publications and CD-ROMS, Gale currently offers 86 databases, providing information in many fields, including biography, history, literary criticism, literature, poetry, and science. School and public libraries may have some of the following databases that focus on history, literature, and current issues.
	American Journey—Includes 15 separate databases covering such topics as African-American Experience, the Revolution, Civil War, Vietnam Era, and World War I and the Jazz Age. Provides several thousand primary source materials, including documents, diaries, letters, and speeches, as well as essays, biographies, photos, maps, and audio and video clips.
	Biography Resource Center—Provides more than 400,000 biographies of over 315,000 people from around the world. Combines 100 Gale databases with over 250 full-text periodicals.
	Contemporary Authors—Provides current biographical and bibliographical data on over 120,000 modern American and international authors. Covers fiction, nonfiction, poetry, and drama, with biweekly updates.
	Contemporary Literary Criticism Select—An extensive collection of critical essays on contemporary writers. Includes introductions, biographies, lists of principal works, and sources for further study.
	Discovering Collection—combines the content and resources from **DISCovering Authors, DISCovering U.S. History, DISCovering Science**, and **DISCovering Biography**, and from the **Junior Reference Collection**. Includes over 45,000 essays, overviews, critical analyses, biographies, timelines, and multimedia elements.
	Literature Resource Center—A collection of 371,000 full-text articles from 230 literary journals. Includes critical essays, overviews, plot summaries, explications, biographies, and portraits.
	Opposing Viewpoints Resource Center—Information that supports contrasting positions about contemporary issues such as censorship, drugs and athletes, illegal immigrants, pornography, teenage sexual behavior, and terrorism. Includes magazine and newspaper articles, statistics, current events topics, and overviews. Uses Greenhaven Press publications and other sources.
	Twayne's Authors Series—Combines the contents of over 600 books. Provides information about individual authors in the U.S., England, and the world, as well as thematic and chronological topics.
	U.S. History Resource Center—A source of historical data from 1900 to the present. It provides information from 23 reference sources, 1000 original documents, and over 90 journals and periodicals as well as radio and TV transcripts. Includes a useful Research Guide and Search Tips. There is also a Modern World History Resource Center.
Greenwood Authors 4 Teens http://www.authors4teens.com	Provides information about contemporary authors whose books explore teenage life, e.g., Don Gallo, Norma Fox Mazer, Walter Dean Myers, and Paul Zindel. Includes biographies, lengthy interviews, and current information.

Online Content Services—Subscription-Based	
Source	**Description**
McGraw-Hill Encyclopedia of Science and Technology Online http://www.accessscience.com	Includes over 8000 articles, dictionary terms, research updates, 2000 biographies of leading scientists, and late-breaking news about discoveries in the world of science and technology.
PsycARTICLES http://proquest.umi.com/login	A database of full-text articles from journals published by the American Psychological Association and from 50 other psychology publications covering human physiology, and personality, social, and educational psychology, from 1992 to the present.

Table 4

Other Online Services—By Subscription	
Source	**Description**
Associated Press Wide World Photo Archive http://www.apwideworld.com	An online collection of multimedia material, including a wide selection of photos and images dating from the 1840s, from the print and negative library of the Associated Press. Includes over 800,000 photos as well as charts, graphs, tables, and maps.

2.   Other Libraries

After starting your search for information in the media center at your school, it's wise to check out other libraries before searching the Internet. Public and university libraries may have databases that your school does not have, and they may have other resources as well.

- Your **local public library**, whether it is a town, city, or county facility, may be especially useful if you are investigating local history, for example, a house in town that was a stop on the Underground Railroad, or a local veteran who organized demonstrations against the Vietnam War. From your school media center, you may be able to access the catalog of titles in your public library. But you will probably want to go there in person, to browse and to talk to staff members, as well as to arrange to borrow the books you need. Many libraries can borrow books from other libraries.

- A **university library** is another valuable resource, if there is one nearby. Although many university libraries restrict circulation privileges to their own students and staff, you can often read and photocopy material that you find there. You can search college and university library catalogs on the Internet, and sometimes the media center staff at your school can arrange interlibrary loans.

3. The World Wide Web on the Internet

By using the World Wide Web on the Internet, you will be able to find the latest developments that affect your topic, whether it is about bone cancer research, critical response to the Mel Gibson movie <u>The Passion of the Christ</u>, an earthquake in Iran, or political unrest in Zimbabwe. But there are millions of documents out there, and searching for the right ones can be painfully time-consuming. There are books and Web sites to assist you in this endeavor, and all the search engines provide a help button as well. Because search engines and Web sites keep changing, detailed information about them is on pages 219-230 in Appendix D. Here are a few tips that will speed your search.

Ten Tips for Searching the Internet

Tip 1.   **Have a clear research plan or strategy.**
Before you begin an Internet search, make sure that you've defined the question you're trying to answer. Keep your topic narrow, but consider more than one approach. For example, if you want to explore the problems of teacher evaluation, you can focus on training, testing, or merit pay. You can limit your study to elementary, secondary, or college education; you can look at publications from the past year, decade, or century.

Tip 2.   **Choose your keyword or keywords with care.**
They should identify your topic precisely. If necessary, try using synonyms and alternative spellings.

Tip 3.   **Use your school media center subscription databases to start.**
Start by searching in the databases that your school media center subscribes to, for example, SIRS, ProQuest, or Gale. These sites provide reliable information from reputable authorities. The editors and compilers have selected documents that are especially useful to high school researchers, and they have excluded irresponsible or irrelevant material.

Tip 4.   **Use sites that focus on a specific area.**
Next, before searching the whole Internet, go to respected, highly regarded sites that focus on a specific area, for example, THOMAS, National Library of Medicine, EDGAR, NASA, and ERIC.

Tip 5.   **Review Appendix D: Search Engines.**
Review the information on pages 219-230 in Appendix D under Search Engines, and select the ones best suited for your particular project. Pay attention to the specific ways to narrow your search using a particular search engine. Don't fixate on one search engine—different engines turn up surprisingly different results.

Tip 6.   **Use advanced or power searches.**
Remember that most search engines offer advanced or power searches. They also provide a help menu.

Tip 7.   **Bookmark helpful sites.**
Bookmarking sites that you find most helpful makes it easy to find them again.

Tip 8.   **Stay focused and stick to your topic.**
It's easy to become distracted and to spend hours on surfing that is amusing but nonproductive.

Tip 9.   **Be flexible.**
If a thorough search using your original keywords does not produce good results, try changing them. "Affirmative Action" and "Racial Quotas" yield quite different results, as do "Agent Orange" and "Effects of Agent Orange."

Tip 10.   **Evaluate the sites you find.**
Remember that not all sites are equal, that is, equally reliable. You must constantly evaluate the sites you find. Always determine the source of the information they offer. Quoting from a sixth grader's biography of Jules Verne, complete with errors in spelling and grammar, that a teacher has posted on the school's Web page, won't help you produce an A+ research paper.

Other Ways to Use the Internet

- **Talk with experts.**

  You no longer have to live next door to an expert to talk about your research. With e-mail and searches on the World Wide Web, you can be in touch with experts all over the world, either by corresponding with them directly or by reading on their home pages about their latest work. A number of Web sites can help you find someone with expertise in your field, including Facsnet: Sources Online (http://facsnet.org) and Profnet (www3.profnet.com).

- **Talk with others who share your interest.**

  They may not be experts, but they are often passionately interested in a particular subject, whether it is snow boarding, child rearing, Stephen King, or Renaissance music. You can join a subject-related listserv, which is a mailing list, or you can drop in on a Usenet newsgroup to discuss your topic and hear a variety of opinions, ranging from highly expert to totally misinformed. To participate in a listserv, you must first subscribe; messages go to your e-mail box. Listservs often provide useful anecdotal information. For example, if you were researching memory loss, you might want to lurk, that is, eavesdrop, for a while on a listserv for people interested in the care of patients with Alzheimer's disease. A caution: it's best not to give your home address or phone number when chatting online.

Warning: Two Internet pitfalls

1. **Mistaking a netmyth for a confirmable truth**

   Although the Internet is a marvelous source of information, you must use it with caution. As W. H. Earle points out in an article in the <u>Baltimore Sun</u>, any crank or dingbat can set up a home page or post messages that contain lies, errors, and absurdities. Be sure to check the reliability of your Internet sources, and find other sources to confirm information from the Net. For help in evaluating a Web site, check the evaluation form on pages 231-232 in Appendix D. And think twice before you confidently assert that Microsoft has taken over the Vatican.

2. **Submitting something found on the Internet as your own original work**

   Because you can find wonderful essays, scientific papers, literary analyses, critical reviews, and reports on the Internet, the temptation may be great to take a short cut and turn in a ready-made item instead of pursuing your research plan and completing your own paper. The proliferation of electronic term paper mills also encourages academic dishonesty. But you should remember that the penalties for plagiarism are severe; the techniques for discovering it have become increasingly sophisticated; and the familiarity of teachers with helpful sites like SparkNotes probably exceeds that of students. Above all, you want to keep your honor and your self-respect.

Summary

Finding Sources

- The chief resources for student researchers are the school media center, public and university libraries, and the Internet.

- Most libraries offer print, nonprint, electronic, and human resources.

- The major electronic resources are information databases, online reference books, and subscription-based online services for various academic disciplines.

- Following a few simple rules will facilitate an Internet search.

- One can also use e-mail, electronic mailing lists, and Usenet newsgroups to obtain information from the Internet.

- Consult Appendix D for information about search engines and useful Web sites.

Chapter 4
Topic Selection.

Now that you've learned your way around your school's media center, you're ready to choose a topic for your paper. In the best of all possible worlds, any topic would be acceptable: marriage between transgendered persons, soap operas, skateboarding, the latest Tom Clancy novel, or intergalactic travel. Unfortunately, usually teachers must impose limitations because they need to pay attention to specific course requirements, curriculum objectives, or departmental stipulations. Teachers sometimes assign topics, but more often, they provide a list of acceptable topics, from which you can choose the one you find most fascinating. With luck, you'll be able to indulge your curiosity and investigate a subject that intrigues you, anything from Buddhist ethics to Mesopotamian pottery to road building in Tanzania. This chapter explains five steps that will make topic selection easier.

Step 1. **Select an excellent topic.** This means one that:

- Genuinely interests you.
- Is consistent with the purpose of the assignment.
- Shows awareness of the intended audience.
- Is sufficiently narrow for a project of the length and form assigned, for example, a five-minute oral presentation, videotape, slide show, poster session, or debate.
- Is not too technical, that is, does not depend on the audience's knowledge of advanced nuclear physics.
- Is not trivial, e.g., whether Cherry Garcia is a better ice cream flavor than Chunky Monkey.
- Is not exceedingly vague or general, for example, the meaning of life or the causes of world conflict.

Step 2. **Narrow your topic and find an angle.** It's a good idea to:

- Consult your teacher to make sure that your topic is suitable.
- Heed any special requirements for the assignment. Does it call for a position paper, a comparison, a causal analysis, a solution to a problem, or an op-ed piece? An op-ed piece is an opinion column such as those that appear on the page opposite the editorial page in newspapers like the New York Times or the Washington Post.
- Find an approach that will distinguish your paper from 25 others.

- Focus on a specific aspect of the topic instead of trying to deal with a large general subject.
- Look in Chapter 5 for more information on this subject.

Step 3.   **Do some serious preliminary work.** This may include:

- Reading articles in general encyclopedias or other reference works.
- Consulting librarians and other local experts.
- Using the Internet, databases, CD-ROMs, other electronic sources, vertical files, and the like.
- Making sure that adequate resources are available for researching your topic.
- Trying a variety of approaches to your topic. Look at the topic from different angles. For example:

  a. Koalas

  - ▸ Threats to their survival (cause)
  - ▸ Differences from bears (comparison, classification)
  - ▸ Reasons for their highly specialized diet (cause)

  b. Global Warming

  - ▸ Controversy over evidence of recent climate change
  - ▸ Causes of global warming (cause)
  - ▸ Dangerous consequences (effect)
  - ▸ Solutions to the problem

  c. The Battle of Britain

  - ▸ Differences from other World War II battles (comparison)
  - ▸ Effect on the outcome of the war (effect)
  - ▸ Reasons for the Allies' defeat of the Axis (cause, process)

Step 4.   **Brainstorm.** This may consist of:

- Jotting down ideas or making a rough outline.
- Doing a concept webbing or branching diagram, where you write down as many ideas as possible that connect with the subject.
- Freewriting (also called fastwriting) to generate a flow of ideas about your topic.
- Letting your thoughts percolate for a while.

Step 5. **Ask questions about your subject.** When you find a question that intrigues you, you can turn it into a tentative thesis statement. Here are some examples.

General subject: The Role of American Women in World War II

Possible research questions:
- Why were American women not drafted into the army?
- Why were they excluded from combat duty?
- What kinds of jobs were available in defense industries?
- In what ways could women volunteer for military service?
- Could they find work as spies, couriers, or cryptographers?
- Under what conditions could women pilot aircraft?
- In what ways did women aid the war effort?
- What were the consequences for women when military personnel came home after the war ended?
- How did World War II affect women's demands for equal rights?

General subject: Substance Abuse with Inhalants

Possible research questions:
- What are the chief products that inhalant abusers use, and why are these products sought?
- What is the extent of inhalant abuse, and why has there been an increase?
- What are the short-term effects of inhalant abuse?
- What are the long-term effects?
- Why do some children become inhalant addicts?
- What programs are available to help inhalant abusers?
- How can inhalant abuse be prevented?

Summary

Topic Selection

A good topic for a research paper is:

- Fascinating to you.
- Narrow enough to be manageable within the page limit.
- Not too technical.
- Not trivial.
- Specific and concrete.
- Researchable, that is, not dependent entirely on personal convictions or late-breaking news.

Chapter 5
Narrowing the Topic

The focus of this chapter is narrowing your topic, a crucial step in writing a successful research paper. You should spend extra time and thought on this task, as it requires quite a bit of preliminary reading. Doing a good job here will also save you from taking voluminous notes that turn out to be useless because they are not on target.

Below are three examples that illustrate different methods of trimming a topic down to manageable size.

Method 1 A good way to start narrowing your topic is to ask at least five searching questions about your general subject. A student interested in football might ask:

- How has the game changed since its inception?
- How did football originate?
- How dangerous is it? Is it becoming more dangerous?
- What is the secret of being successful in pro football?
- How has equipment changed to make the game safer?

Any one of these questions can lead to a workable, narrowed topic that the writer can turn into a thesis statement, as Chapter 6 shows.

Method 2 Another way to narrow your topic is to break the general subject into smaller parts by looking at it from different angles. A student considering the topic of social criticism in Charles Dickens's novels might use these strategies:

- Concentrate on one novel rather than several. This might yield:

  a. Dickens's attitude toward the imprisonment of debtors in <u>David Copperfield</u>.

  b. Dickens's portrayal of child labor in <u>David Copperfield</u>.

- Focus on a particular problem or aspect:

  a. Dickens's criticism of the judicial system in <u>Bleak House</u>.

   b. Dickens's fears about the danger of revolution in <u>A Tale of Two Cities</u>.

- Look at the major elements in the novel–plot, characterization, setting, theme, style, structure, etc. Focusing on the theme of self-discovery in <u>Great Expectations</u> could help you to zero in on a topic that you can handle in a paper of three to five pages.

- Compare or contrast two Dickens novels that share important elements, for example, attitude toward the abuse of children in <u>David Copperfield</u> and <u>Oliver Twist</u>.

Method 3   Many historical events, like the Treaty of Versailles or the struggle to establish a Jewish homeland, are so complicated that you cannot deal with them adequately in a single paper. But you can focus on a specific aspect or take an unusual approach.

For instance, for the Treaty of Versailles:

- Prepare diary entries for one of the major participants: Woodrow Wilson, Georges Clemenceau, or Vittorio Emanuele Orlando.

- Debate the validity of a selected few of the most important points in Wilson's Fourteen Points.

- Analyze the major problems confronting the negotiators.

- Write an editorial sympathizing with Germany's dissatisfaction with the treaty.

- Assess the consequences of this dissatisfaction.

- Write a speech opposing or encouraging American participation in the League of Nations.

If the struggle to establish a Jewish state in Palestine fascinates you, you might narrow your topic in one of the following ways:

- Create letters written by the leaders of political Zionism, Theodor Herzl or Chaim Weizmann, about the problems they faced.

- Recreate the debate in the British Cabinet concerning the release of the Balfour Declaration of 1917.

- Write a speech expressing Arab opposition to a Jewish homeland and concern for Palestinians' rights.

- Focus on the role of the League of Nations or the United Nations.

- Give an eyewitness account of the first World Zionist Congress in Basel.

- Discuss the influence on Zionism of anti-Semitism in France (Dreyfus Affair) or in Russia (Kishinev pogrom).

Summary

Narrowing the Topic

To narrow a topic:

- Ask questions about a general subject.

- Focus on a single issue or theme in a writer's work.

- Focus on a single work, or a single aspect, e.g., characterization.

- Look for a specific approach to a historical event: cause or effect, comparison or contrast, or process analysis. Break a large historical movement into smaller parts; focus on a key individual, turning point, or opposing force.

Chapter 6
Formulating a Thesis Statement

There are several approaches to the selection of a thesis statement. Your teacher may give you total freedom to choose, with or without help; he or she may ask you to select a thesis statement from a limited set; or your teacher may assign you a specific, pre-written thesis statement. If you formulate your own, your teacher will usually ask you to submit your thesis statement for approval before you start to write your paper. This chapter deals with the latter situation, where you must write your own thesis statement.

Procedure for Arriving at a Satisfactory Thesis Statement

Step 1.   Begin by examining the general topic for angles, aspects, or approaches, as the chapters on Topic Selection and Topic Narrowing explain (Chapters 4 and 5). **Do some preliminary reading to get ideas.** Write down some questions about your topic.

Step 2.   Select an angle that narrows the topic to manageable proportions.

Step 3.   Propose a judgment, criticism, or evaluation that you can support in a paper of the prescribed length. This is **a temporary, tentative thesis statement**, one that you will later refine and improve.

Step 4.   Determine how you will **back up** your thesis statement by deciding what topics will support it, that is, what topics will provide evidence, reasons, and arguments that will convince the reader of the soundness of your thesis statement.

A good thesis statement is:

- **A declarative sentence** that states clearly and concisely the main point that the author wishes to make.

> The perceived injustices of the Treaty of Versailles made it a major cause of World War II.

- **Usually a sentence that embodies a judgment, evaluation, or criticism,** often apparent in its use of value terms, e.g., good, better, best, valuable, worthwhile, desirable, favorable, major, most important, effective, significant, insightful, or should.

  > The major problems that made enforcement of the Treaty of Versailles difficult concerned disarmament, reparations, and the punishment of war criminals.

- **A statement you consider significant,** so that if someone says, "So what?" you can answer that question.

A good thesis statement <u>may</u> also:

- **Suggest a comparison or a contrast.**

  > The treaty that followed World War II was radically different from the one that concluded World War I.

- **Focus primarily on the causes or effects of a particular event, condition, or change.**

  > A number of economic and political developments in Europe made World War I almost inevitable.

- **Propose a solution to a problem or recommend a policy.**

  > Community service should be mandatory for all high school students, but it should take place during the school day.

Remember—a good thesis statement <u>is not</u>:

- ☹ **A statement of fact.**

  > The Treaty of Versailles was signed by the four major powers and became effective January 1920.

- ☹ **Merely the expression of a personal opinion.**

  > I think the Treaty of Versailles was a foolish mistake.

- ☹ **A vague generalization.**

  > The Treaty of Versailles caused the world a lot of problems.

- ☹ **A question.**

  > Was the Treaty of Versailles a major force in precipitating World War II?

Examples of good thesis statements

The examples below show how the writer moves from general subject to narrowed topic to precise thesis statement.

General subject: Teenage runaways

Specific topic: Reasons why adolescents run away from home

Thesis statement: Many adolescents run away from home, not because of delinquent activity but because they are seeking help.

General subject: History of the Jewish people

Specific topic: The attempt to establish a Jewish homeland

Thesis statement: American Zionists played an important role in the struggle to establish a Jewish homeland.

General subject: Euthanasia

Specific topic: Arguments opposing the practice of euthanasia

Thesis statement: Within the Judeo-Christian tradition, there are strong religious arguments against euthanasia.

General subject: The electromagnetic spectrum

Specific topic: Use of X-rays in the analysis of paintings

Thesis statement: Radiography makes possible the verification of paintings by revealing age and underlying brushstroke techniques.

Summary

Formulating a Thesis Statement

An excellent thesis statement is:

- A judgment, criticism, or evaluation that research can support.
- A declarative sentence that states the main point of the essay.
- Something worth saying.
- Not a statement of fact, a personal opinion, a vague generalization, or a question.

Chapter 7
Supporting a Thesis Statement

Once you have formulated your thesis statement, you are ready to tackle the subject of this chapter: finding topics to support it. You need to do this before you start taking notes. Figuring out how to support your thesis statement will help you to put useful topic headings on your note cards, to distinguish relevant from irrelevant material, and to know where to put the relevant material. A coherent rough draft requires systematic note taking as a preliminary step.

Procedure

After turning your topic into a tentative thesis statement, divide your narrowed topic into three or more major topics that provide support for your thesis, that is, evidence or arguments that will convince the reader that your thesis is valid.

Example: To support the thesis statement that throughout history, dogs have been useful to mankind in many ways, Chris first listed some ways that dogs have served humans:

- *Hunting and tracking*
- *Guarding and attacking*
- *Sniffing out drugs or bombs*
- *Acting as guide dogs for the blind*
- *Providing companionship*
- *Pulling sleds in snowy regions*
- *Finding victims in collapsed buildings*
- *Herding sheep and other farm animals*

From these, she selected the three that she found most interesting. She made sure they were promising as major topics, that is, topics about which she expects to find plenty of information to provide examples, details, facts, statistics, and excellent quotations. She chose:

> A. Hunting
>
> B. Guiding
>
> C. Providing companionship

As she did her research and note taking, she found another promising topic, which she added as a subtopic to b.—aiding the deaf by recognizing sounds like the doorbell or phone. Notice that topics a., b., and c. all support Chris's thesis statement: they provide reasons or arguments for accepting it.

As you will recall, these supporting arguments are called your Method of Development (MOD). As further examples, here are several students' thesis statements and topics that support them.

Thesis statement: Women's basketball has changed radically since the game was introduced at Smith College in 1892.

> A. Court size and restricted playing areas
>
> B. Limitations on running, dribbling, and reaching in
>
> C. Other rules of the game
>
> D. Players' clothing

Thesis statement: Dolphins are highly intelligent creatures that share several abilities with humans.

> A. Imitation, memorization
>
> B. Foresight, learning from observation, communicating experience
>
> C. Solving complex problems, performing elaborate tasks

Thesis statement: There are many serious threats to dolphins' continued survival in the world today.

> A. Outright hunting
>
> B. Getting caught in tuna nets
>
> C. Others: Pollution? Decline in food supply? Changing environment?

Thesis statement: There seem to be some negative, long-term consequences of marijuana smoking, but the evidence is inconclusive.

     A. *Alteration of attention*

     B. *Memory impairment*

     C. *Physical addiction*

     D. *Increased risk of lung cancer*

Thesis statement: Loneliness and alienation are dominant themes in the fiction of J. D. Salinger.

     A. *Isolation from family*

     B. *Isolation from individuals*

     C. *Isolation from society and institutions*

Thesis statement: Although they tell the same story, Charles Dickens's novel <u>Oliver Twist</u> and the popular musical <u>Oliver!</u> differ in several important ways.

     A. *Length and complexity*

     B. *Realism*

     C. *Dramatic impact*

     D. *Social criticism*

Thesis statement: Cheating has been part of professional baseball in the United States since the first game was played in 1871.

     A. *Tampering with equipment*

     B. *Dishonest groundskeeping*

     C. *Using illegal devices to steal signals*

Summary

Supporting a Thesis Statement

To find support for your thesis statement:

- Write down your tentative thesis statement.

- List as many supporting topics as you can.

- Select the three or four that seem most promising.

- Do preliminary reading to locate supporting information for your major topics.

- As you read, add or drop major topics, depending on what you find.

Chapter 8
Creating a Topic Outline

This chapter shows how the outline fits into the research process. The key points about an outline are:

- It provides the **structure** for your paper.

- It allows you to see **relationships** among main ideas and supporting facts.

- It **changes**. You should keep revising your outline as your research and writing progress so that it reflects new insights, deletions, modifications, connections, and improvements.

- It is finished only when your paper is finished. Then you can write it in cement.

First, let's review the steps up to this point.

Review	
Step 1.	Find an appealing topic within your general subject area.
Step 2.	Narrow it by finding a specific angle or approach.
Step 3.	Locate sources of information about your topic; record information on source cards.
Step 4.	Formulate a tentative thesis statement that states the central idea of your paper.
Step 5.	Determine the major topics that will support your thesis statement. These become the main topics in your outline; they are also the topic headings on your note cards.

Preliminary Topic Outline

Now, take a look at the sample topic outline below. It is the skeleton that you will fill in as you continue with your research.

Thesis Statement

A. First Major Supporting Topic
1. Specific examples, details
2. Specific examples, details
3. Specific examples, details

B. Second Major Supporting Topic
1. Specific examples, details
2. Specific examples, details
3. Specific examples, details

C. Third Major Supporting Topic
1. Specific examples, details
2. Specific examples, details
3. Specific examples, details

Here's an example of the way one student formulated a thesis statement and determined the major topics of support.

First, Jon wrote a tentative thesis statement about the dangers of professional football.

Then, based on his knowledge of the sport and on some preliminary reading, he decided to try these supporting topics:

A. Head injuries
B. Shoulder and spinal cord injuries
C. Knee injuries, leg fractures

Finally, he wrote down his thesis statement and entered his major topics on the outline opposite A, B, and C. Later, after he does his research, he will fill in a brief list of examples, facts, quotations, and the like that he will use in his paper. He will enter them under each major topic, using the numbers provided. He may also find another major topic, for example, injuries resulting from artificial turf.

Of course, Jon may find so much information about head injuries that he will decide to limit his essay just to concussions suffered by quarterbacks. In that case, he'll change his thesis statement and revise his topics. Since writing a research paper is an exploration, it's not surprising that the writer often ends up in an unexpected place.

This is what Jon's preliminary outline looks like:

Thesis statement: Despite efforts to improve safety through rules and equipment changes, professional football is a violent game that causes many serious injuries.

    A. Head injuries [major topic – also heading on note cards]

        1. Statistical or numerical evidence—the incidence of head injuries in the National Football League.

        2. Quotation from Dr. Robert Cantu, medical director of the National Center for Catastrophic Sports Injury Research in Chapel Hill, NC.

        3. Example: Drew Bledsoe, Buffalo Bills quarterback, who has suffered multiple concussions.

    B. Shoulder and spinal cord injuries [major topic and heading on note cards]

        1.

        2.

        3.

    C. Knee injuries [major topic and heading on note cards]

        1.

        2.

        3.

Points to Remember

Point 1 Look for supporting facts, statistics, details, examples, and quotations, under your major topics, in this case,

    A. Head injuries

    B. Shoulder and spinal cord injuries

    C. Knee injuries

Point 2 Remember that these are also the headings or slugs at the top of your note cards. It is sometimes useful to add subheadings to your note cards. For example, head injuries might subdivide into **Injuries to quarterbacks** and **Injuries to other players**.

Point 3 Change your topics, add another category, or substitute a different one, if you wish. The number of major topics is not fixed. There are often more than three.

Point 4 The number of subtopics is also not fixed, but you would never have fewer than two under a given topic. Under **Head Injuries**, for example, you might find information about concussions suffered by quarterbacks Joe Montana, Steve Young, Chris Miller, Stan Humphries, and Troy Aikman. These topics each support the claim that football is dangerous.

Point 5 Strive for logic, consistency, and completeness in your outline. Make your lettering and indenting reflect the logical relationship among the ideas: the major topics are the chief support for the thesis statement, and the subtopics and details provide further support in the form of facts, quotations, statistics, and examples.

Point 6 A topic outline, rather than a full-sentence outline, is usually sufficient for most research essays. Check with your teacher. The preliminary outline is a bare-bones, tentative indication of how the paper will shape up. The final outline reflects the changes that occurred in your thinking as your research progressed, and it shows exactly the structure of the final product. See Appendix A for examples of final outlines for two kinds of research papers.

Summary

Creating a Topic Outline

Topic outlines:

- Make clear the structure of your paper.

- Show how supporting topics and subtopics connect to your thesis statement.

- Remind you that the **topic headings** on your note cards should match the **major topics** in your outline.

- Change during the research process.

- Are exemplified in Appendix A.

Source Cards—MLA

Source card for a book

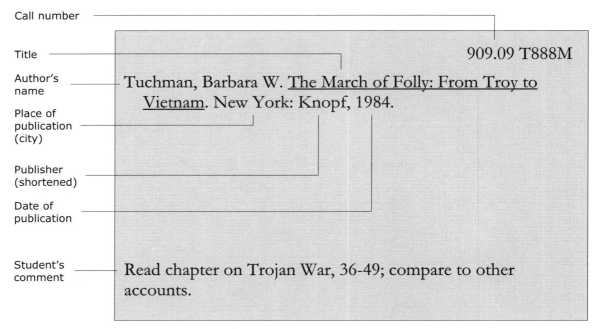

Call number

Title

Author's name

Place of publication (city)

Publisher (shortened)

Date of publication

Student's comment

909.09 T888M

Tuchman, Barbara W. The March of Folly: From Troy to Vietnam. New York: Knopf, 1984.

Read chapter on Trojan War, 36-49; compare to other accounts.

Source card for an article

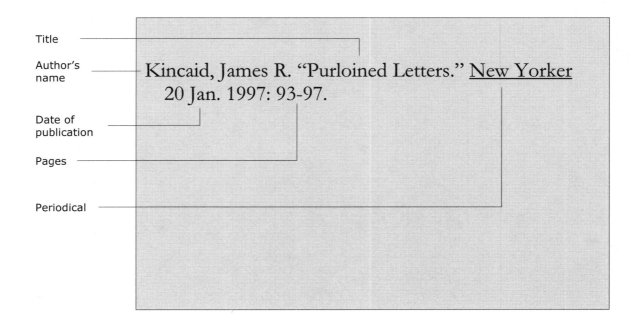

Title

Author's name

Date of publication

Pages

Periodical

Kincaid, James R. "Purloined Letters." New Yorker 20 Jan. 1997: 93-97.

Chapter 9A
Source Cards
MLA

This chapter explains **source cards, the most convenient way to record the publication information about your sources.** Of course, you could record this information on scraps of paper, on the back of your hand, in your notebook, or on small paper airplanes; but experienced writers find a more systematic approach works better.

First, study the diagram of model source cards on the facing page, noting the information provided and its arrangement. Then read over carefully the steps in the process. This chapter uses the form approved by the Modern Language Association (MLA); the next chapter uses that of the American Psychological Association (APA). A note at the end of Chapter 1 explains these organizations.

Step 1. Review Chapter 3, which discusses the resources available for research.

Notice the great variety of sources of information now found in computerized catalogs: books, magazines, videos, audiotapes, microfiche, microfilm, reference works, etc. There are electronic sources too numerous to list that include online databases, newspaper indexes, and CD-ROM programs.

If your school media center specialists provide orientation for specific research projects, listen carefully; it can save you hours of fruitless searching.

Step 2. When you locate an information source that looks promising, **use a pen** and lined 3x5 index cards (source cards) to record the information. Put it in exactly the form that you will need later for your works cited page, the page at the end of your paper where you list all the sources that you actually used. Study the models before you write, and use them later to check for accuracy. Notice that the correct form for source cards and for entries on your works cited page is the same.

Step 3. Record the following information on each card. Look at the examples at the end of this chapter to see the exact form of each entry.

a. Call number, if available, in upper right corner.

b. Author's full name, last name first; include middle initial if used.

    c. Title of book, in italics or underlined; or title of article, in quotation marks.

    d. For a book: place of publication, that is, the city (no state); for cities outside the U.S., give the country only if omitting it would result in ambiguity; publisher, in short form; date of publication, usually the same as the copyright date. If several cities are given, use only the first one, and use only the latest date given.

    e. For an article in a periodical, magazine, or newspaper, include also the date and pages. Consult the model for order, capitalization, and punctuation.

    f. For electronic sources, note the form provided in Chapter 20A.

    g. For other sources, including letters, films, artwork, and the like, see Chapter 20A.

    h. For a book with a subtitle, list it as part of the title, joining it to the main title with a colon. For example, where the title of the book is <u>F. Scott Fitzgerald</u> and the subtitle is <u>A Collection of Critical Essays</u>, write the whole title as follows: <u>F. Scott Fitzgerald: A Collection of Critical Essays.</u>

    i. Indent the second line and subsequent lines of the entry five spaces or one-half inch.

Step 4. Add your own critical comments, suggestions, or reminders, either at the bottom of the card or on the back. Although most teachers make this step optional, it is often useful to jot down the numbers of pages, chapters, or sections that look promising.

Step 5. If your teacher requires it, hand in your source cards for checking. Teachers expect your cards to be in ink and to contain complete information in the correct form, including spelling, punctuation, and capitalization.

Step 6. If your cards are returned with comments or errors noted, make the necessary corrections immediately. Keep your cards in a safe place. Small Ziploc plastic bags are useful for carrying cards about.

When you finish writing the final version of your paper, alphabetize the cards for the sources **you actually used**, and prepare your works cited page, using the information on your cards. Consult Chapter 20A, Works Cited, and note the model provided.

Summary

Source Cards—MLA

Source cards:

- Record publication information required for accurate documentation.

- Match exactly the form of entries on your works cited page.

- Require a pen, 3x5 index cards, and accuracy in recording.

- Require specific information in proper form, whether your source is a book, periodical, electronic database, or other online location. See Chapter 20A for details about specific entries.

Sample Source Cards—MLA

"Gay Marriage Will Be 'Litmus Test' in
   Elections, Says Religious Right." Church
   & State Jan. 2004: 19.
   ProQuest Platinum. 30 Jan. 2004
   <http://proquest.umi.com/login>.

Periodical article in online database

                                        B
                                   Boswell
Martin, Peter. A Life of James Boswell. New
   Haven: Yale UP, 2000.

Look up the account of Boswell's trip to the
   Hebrides.

Book published by a university press.

                              814.54
                              BOO
Herbert, A. P. "About Bathrooms." The Book of
   20th Century Essays. Ed. Ian Hamilton. New
   York: Fromm, 2000. 59-62.

Essay in an anthology

Valera, Juan. Pepita Jimenez. Vol. 20, Part 1.
   Harvard Classics Shelf of Fiction. New
   York: Collier, 1917. Bartleby.com:Great
   Books Online. Ed. Steven van Leeuwen.
   2004. 30 Jan. 2004
   <http://www.bartleby.com/320/1/202/html>.

Online book

Milton, Katharine. "Something to Howl About."
   Natural History Oct. 2003: 20-24.

Article in a magazine

One Flew over the Cuckoo's Nest. Screenplay
   by Lawrence Hauben and Bo Goldman,
   based on the novel by Ken Kesey. Dir. Milos
   Forman. Perf. Jack Nicholson, Louise
   Fletcher, William Redfield. DVD. Fantasy
   Films, 1997.

Note specific ways the movie differs from the
   novel.

Film on DVD

Source Cards—APA

Source card for a book

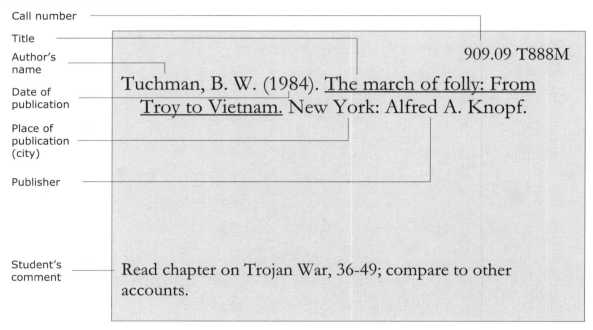

Call number

Title

Author's name

Date of publication

Place of publication (city)

Publisher

Student's comment

909.09 T888M

Tuchman, B. W. (1984). The march of folly: From Troy to Vietnam. New York: Alfred A. Knopf.

Read chapter on Trojan War, 36-49; compare to other accounts.

Source card for an article

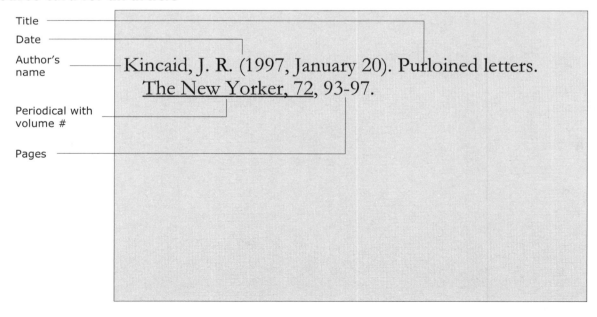

Title

Date

Author's name

Periodical with volume #

Pages

Kincaid, J. R. (1997, January 20). Purloined letters. The New Yorker, 72, 93-97.

Chapter 9B
Source Cards
APA

This chapter explains **source cards, the most convenient way to record the information you find about the sources of material for your paper.** Of course, you could record this information on scraps of paper, on the back of your hand, in your notebook, or on small paper airplanes; but experienced writers find a more systematic approach works better.

First, study the diagram of model source cards on the facing page, noting the information provided and its arrangement. Then read over carefully the steps in the process. This chapter uses the form approved by the American Psychological Association (APA). A note at the end of Chapter 1 explains this organization.

Step 1.   Read Chapter 3, which discusses the resources available for research.

- Notice the great variety of sources of information now found in computerized catalogs: books, magazines, videos, audiotapes, reference works, etc. There are electronic sources too numerous to list that include online databases, newspaper indexes, and CD-ROM programs.

- If your school media center specialists provide orientation for specific research projects, listen carefully; it can save you hours of fruitless searching.

Step 2.   When you locate an information source that looks promising, **use a pen** and lined 3x5 index cards (source cards), and record the information on the card. Put it in exactly the form that you will need later for your reference list, the page at the end of your paper where you list the sources you actually used. Study the models before you write, and use them later to check for accuracy. Notice that the correct form for source cards and for entries on your references page is the same.

Step 3.   Record the following information on each card. Look at the examples at the end of this chapter to see the exact form of each entry, and check Chapter 20B before you write.

        a. Call number, if available, in upper right corner.

        b. Author's surname first; use initials for first and middle names.

c. Publication date, in parentheses (year, month, day).

d. Title of book, underlined; or title of article, not underlined or in quotation marks. The APA prefers italics in the final version, but on your source cards you will need to underline. Capitalize as follows: Capitalize the first word, the first word after a dash or colon, and proper nouns. Do not capitalize the second word of a hyphenated compound.

e. For a book, place of publication, that is, the city and state for U.S. publishers; add the country for publishers outside the United States. Omit the state for cities that are well known for publishing: Baltimore, Boston, Chicago, Los Angeles, New York, Philadelphia, and San Francisco. Use the official two-letter U.S. Postal Service abbreviations for states. List the publisher, omitting Publishers, Co., or Inc. but retaining Books and Press.

f. For an article in a periodical, magazine, or newspaper, include the volume number and the pages, using arabic numerals. Consult the model for order, capitalization, punctuation, and additional details.

g. For electronic sources, note the form provided in Chapter 20B, Preparing the References.

h. For a book with a subtitle, list it as part of the title, joining it to the main title with a colon. For example, where the title of the book is F. Scott Fitzgerald and the subtitle is A collection of critical essays, write the whole title as follows: F. Scott Fitzgerald: A collection of critical essays.

i. Start your entry at the left margin. Indent the second and all subsequent lines five spaces or one-half inch. This style—the hanging indent—is the preferred form for reference lists. Complete your cards in exactly this form.

Step 4.   Add your own critical comments, suggestions, or reminders, either at the bottom of the card or on the back. Although most teachers make this optional, it is often useful to jot down the numbers of pages, chapters, or sections that look promising.

Step 5.   If your teacher requires it, hand in your source cards for checking. Teachers expect your cards to be in ink and to contain complete information in the correct form, including spelling, punctuation, and capitalization.

Step 6.   If your cards are returned with comments or errors noted, make the necessary corrections immediately, and keep your cards in a safe place. Small Ziploc plastic bags are useful for carrying cards about.

When you finish writing the final version of your paper, alphabetize the cards for the sources **you actually used**, and prepare your references page, using the information on your cards. Consult Chapter 20B on references, and note the model provided.

Summary

Source Cards—APA

Source cards:

- Record publication information required for accurate documentation.

- Match exactly the form of entries on your references page.

- Require a pen, 3x5 index cards, and accuracy in recording.

- Require specific information in proper form, whether your source is a book, periodical, electronic database, or other online location. See Chapter 20B for details about specific entries.

Sample Source Cards—APA

R726.R64 2004

Rosenfeld, B. (2004). Assisted suicide and the right to die: The interface of social science, public policy, and medical ethics. Washington, DC: APA.

Check discussion of moral issues.

Book

Lilienthal, S.O. (1998). Current readings in abnormal psychology: Contemporary questions and debates in psychopathology research. Pacific Grove, CA: Brooks/Cole.

Book

Ashley, S. (2003, October). Artificial muscles. Scientific American, 289, 52-59.

Article in a magazine

Tan, S-H. (2004, January). From cannibalism to empowerment: An Analects-inspired attempt to balance community and liberty. Philosophy East and West, 54. Retrieved February 1, 2004, from ProQuest Platinum database.

Scholarly journal article from online database

Kok, R-M. (2003). Romantic childhood, bourgeois commercialism, and the music of Robert Schumann (Germany). (ATT 3091600). Retrieved February 1, 2004, from ProQuest Digital Dissertations database.

Doctoral dissertation from online database

Westen, D. (1998). The psychoanalytic theory of conflict. Lecture 4 in Is anyone really normal? Perspectives on abnormal psychology. [Cassette recording]. Chantilly, VA: Teaching Company.

Compare to other conflict theories.

Audio recording

Chapter 10
Targeting Useful Information

In this chapter you'll learn about note taking, one of the most time-consuming tasks in the research paper process. Keep in mind this cardinal rule: **The quality of the notes you take is more important than the quantity.** You will need to practice your note taking skills before you can write a successful research paper.

Review

So far, you've completed a number of steps in the research process. You've:

- Found a subject.
- Narrowed it to a manageable topic.
- Formulated a tentative thesis statement.
- Made a topic outline that shows at least three major topics that support your thesis statement.
- Located sources.
- Made source cards.
- Put your hands on actual books and magazines; obtained printouts of articles from electronic databases and other Internet sources.

Now you're staring at the printed page to your left, and a pile of blank note cards to your right. What to do next? Here's an example that will show you how to proceed and will give you some practice.

This is Mark's tentative thesis statement:

Teenagers' excessive consumption of alcohol may cause serious damage to both mind and body.

From his preliminary reading, Mark decided to support his thesis statement with the following two major topics:

1. **Short-term effects**, that is, those evident during and immediately following drinking

2. **Long-term effects**, which subdivide into

        a. Physical effects, i.e., effects on the body

        b. Psychological effects, i.e., effects on the mind and behavior

He plans to concentrate mainly on **long-term effects,** since they struck him as the most serious, but he wants to include such **short-term consequences** as passing out, vomiting, and hangovers. Because these may be more familiar to his audience, Mark figures they might provide a good lead-in for his main discussion.

Mark's next step was to read carefully an article that looked promising. Since it was in a current magazine, he made a photocopy so he could annotate it, that is, underline and make marginal notes. Many students like to use a highlighter for this step because highlighting makes it easier to pick out relevant information later.

Using Mark and his article as a practice exercise, let's go through the steps in the process.

STEP 1.   First, read the first version of the article "Getting Stupid" by Bernice Wuethrich, that appeared in <u>Discover</u>, March 2001, on pages 56-63. It is reprinted at the end of this chapter, starting on page 65. The paragraphs have been numbered for easy reference.

           With a highlighter, pen, or pencil, mark the sections of the article that you think Mark should note for his paper. Remember to look for both **short-term** and **long-term effects,** and for effects on both **body** and **mind.** Ignore other information and details not immediately relevant to these topics.

           Identify your highlighted sections with brief headings and notes. You can use the following abbreviations: ST for Short-term; LT for Long-term; Phys. for Physical; Psych. for Psychological.

STEP 2.   Now read the second version of the same article, which follows the first one. The paragraphs that Mark selected as relevant are highlighted and his notes are in the right margin.

           Notice that he has marked only those paragraphs that contain information about the **effects** of teenage drinking. **He ignored other material in the article, knowing that his note taking must be highly selective. He takes down only what specifically supports his thesis statement.**

STEP 3.   Compare your highlighting with Mark's, and see if you agree. Bear in mind that annotating and highlighting are preliminary steps; you can still change your mind about what you actually write down on your note cards.

Remember that you cannot highlight or annotate in library books and magazines, but you can make copies of pages with useful information and then use a highlighter on your own copy. Using printouts from electronic sources also makes these steps easier.

STEP 4.   List under the topic headings below the information that belongs in each category. Since these are the headings on your note cards, they tell you what information to put on each card.

Short-term Effects (on both mind and body)	Long-term Effects— Physical	Long-term Effects— Psychological
1.	1.	1.
2.	2.	2.
3.	3.	3.
4.		4.
5.		5.
6.		6.
		7.

Future Steps

After copying down the relevant information from this article onto his note cards, Mark will go on to his next source, perhaps an article in Alcoholism: Clinical and Experimental Research or in the American Journal of Psychiatry. For up-to-date information, he might also go to the National Institute on Alcohol Abuse and Alcoholism home page at www.niaaa.nih.gov.

With each new source, he will repeat the procedure, putting the information he finds on additional note cards with the same topic headings: Short-term Effects; Long-term Physical Effects; Long-term Psychological Effects. He will probably put subtopic headings on his note cards, for example, Memory Loss, Attention Deficit, Personality Changes.

If he finds additional effects, he will create another subtopic heading and take down additional information on note cards under that heading. As he records information, he'll add his own comments or questions, keeping them distinct by using braces {. . .}, ink or highlighting of a different color, or some other method to separate source material from his own observations.

Summary

Targeting Useful Information

To locate relevant information before taking notes:

- Identify at least three major topics that support your thesis statement.

- Find a book or magazine with useful material.

- Photocopy the pages of library books or magazines, or print the article from an Internet source.

- Highlight the sentences that support your major topics.

- Make notations in the margins to link the information you found to your topic headings and subheadings.

Getting Stupid
by Bernice Wuethrich

1. *Sarah, a high school senior, drinks in moderation, but many of her friends do not. At one party, a classmate passed out after downing more than 20 shots of hard liquor and had to be rushed to a local emergency room. At another party a friend got sick, so Sarah made her drink water, dressed her in a sweatshirt to keep her warm, and lay her in bed, with a bucket on the floor. Then she brushed the girl's long hair away from her face so that it wouldn't get coated with vomit. "Every weekend, drinking is the only thing people do. Every single party has alcohol," says Sarah. (The names of the teenagers in these stories have been changed to protect their privacy.)*

2. The most recent statistics from the U.S. Substance Abuse and Mental Health Services Administration's National Household Survey on Drug Abuse indicate that nearly 7 million youths between the ages of 12 and 20 binge-drink at least once a month. And despite the fact that many colleges have cracked down on drinking, Henry Wechsler of the Harvard School of Public Health says that two of every five college students still binge-drink regularly. For a male that means downing five or more drinks in a row; for a female it means consuming four drinks in one session at least once in a two-week period.

3. Few teens seem to worry much about what such drinking does to their bodies. Cirrhosis of the liver is unlikely to catch up with them for decades, and heart disease must seem as remote as retirement. But new research suggests that young drinkers are courting danger. Because their brains are still developing well into their twenties, teens who drink excessively may be destroying significant amounts of mental capacity in ways that are more dramatic than in older drinkers.

4. Scientists have long known that excessive alcohol consumption among adults over long periods of time can create brain damage, ranging from a mild loss of motor skills to psychosis and even the inability to form memories. But less has been known about the impact alcohol has on youger brains. Until recently, scientists assumed that a youthful brain is more resilient than an adult brain and could escape many of the worst ills of alcohol. But some researchers are now beginning to question this assumption. Preliminary results from several studies indicate that the younger the brain is, the more it may be at risk. "The adolescent brain is a developing nervous system, and the things you do to it can change it," says Scott Swartzwelder, a neuropsychologist at Duke University and the U.S. Department of Veterans Affairs.

5. Teen drinkers appear to be most susceptible to damage in the hippocampus, a structure buried deep in the brain that is responsible for many types of learning and memory, and the prefrontal cortex, located behind the forehead, which is the brain's chief decision maker and voice of reason. Both areas, especially the prefrontal cortex, undergo dramatic change in the second decade of life.

6. Swartzwelder and his team have been studying how alcohol affects the hippocampus, an evolutionarily old part of the brain that is similar in rats and humans. Six years ago, when Swartzwelder published his first paper suggesting that alcohol disrupts the hippocampus more severely in adolescent rats than in adult rats, "people didn't believe it," he says. Since then, his research has shown that the adolescent brain is more easily damaged in the structures that regulate the acquisition and storage of memories.

7. Learning depends on communication between nerve cells, or neurons, within the hippocampus. To communicate, a neuron fires an electrical signal down its axon, a single fiber extending away from the cell's center. In response, the axon releases chemical messengers, called neurotransmitters, which bind to receptors on the receiving branches of neighboring cells. Depending on the types of neurotransmitters released, the receiving cell may be jolted into action or settle more deeply into rest.

8. But the formation of memories requires more than the simple firing or inhibition of nerve cells. There must be some physical change in the hippocampal neurons that represents the encoding of new information. Scientists believe that this change occurs in the synapses, the tiny gaps between neurons that neurotransmitters traverse. Repeated use of synapses seems to increase their ability to fire up connecting cells. Laboratory experiments on brain tissue can induce this process, called long-term potentiation. Researchers assume that something similar takes place in the intact living brain, although it is impossible to observe directly. Essentially, if the repetitive neural reverberations are strong enough, they burn in new patterns of synaptic circuitry to encode memory, just as the more often a child recites his ABCs, the better he knows them.

9. Swartzwelder's first clue that alcohol powerfully disrupts memory in the adolescent brain came from studying rat hippocampi. He found that alcohol blocks long-term potentiation in adolescent brain tissue much more than in adult tissue. Next, Swartzwelder identified a likely explanation. Long-term potentiation—and thus memory formation—relies in large part on the action of a neurotransmitter known as glutamate, the brain's chemical kingpin of neural excitation. Glutamate strengthens a cell's electrical stimulation when it binds to a docking port called the NMDA receptor. If the receptor is blocked, so is long-term potentiation, and thus memory formation. Swartzwelder found that exposure to the equivalent of just two beers inhibits the NMDA receptors in the hippocampal cells of adolescent rats, while more than twice as much is required to produce the same effect inadult rats. These findings led him to suspect that alcohol consumption might have a dramatic impact on the ability of adolescents to learn. So he set up a series of behavioral tests.

10. First, Swartzwelder's team dosed adolescent and adult rats with alcohol and ran them through maze-learning tests. Compared with the adult rats, the adolescents failed miserably. To see whether similar results held true for humans, Swartzwelder recruited a group of volunteers aged 21 to 29 years old. He couldn't use younger subjects

because of laws that forbid drinking before age 21. He chose to split the volunteers into two groups: 21 to 24 years old and 25 to 29 years old. "While I wouldn't argue that these younger folks are adolescents, even in their early twenties their brains are still developing," Swartzwelder says. After three drinks, with a blood-alcohol level slightly below the National Highway Traffic Safety Administration's recommended limit—.08 percent—the younger group's learning was impaired 25 percent more than the older group's.

11. Intrigued by these results, Swartzwelder's colleague Aaron White, a biological psychologist at Duke, set out to discover how vulnerable the adolescent brain is to long-term damage. He gave adolescent and adult rats large doses of alcohol every other day for 20 days—the equivalent of a 150-pound human chugging 24 drinks in a row. Twenty days after the last binge, when the adolescent rats had reached adulthood, White trained them in a maze-memory task roughly akin to that performed by a human when remembering the location of his car in a parking garage.

12. Both the younger and older rats performed equally well when sober. But when intoxicated, those who had binged as adolescents performed much worse. "Binge alcohol exposure in adolescence appears to produce long-lasting changes in brain function," White says. He suspects that early damage caused by alcohol could surface whenever the brain is taxed. He also suspects that the NMDA receptor is involved, because just as alcohol in the system inhibits the receptor, the drug's withdrawal overstimulates it— which can kill the cell outright.

13. *During the fall semester last year, at least 11 college students died from alcohol related causes—at California State University at Chico, Colgate University in New York, Old Dominion University in Virginia, the University of Michigan, Vincennes University in Kentucky, Washington and Lee University in Virginia, and Washington State University. No one knows how many other students were rushed to emergency rooms for alcohol poisoning, but at Duke, 11 students had visited local ERs in just the first three weeks of school, and in only one night of partying, three students from the University of Tennessee were hospitalized.*

14. Students who drink heavily sometimes joke that they are killing a few brain cells. New research suggests that this is not funny. Some of the evidence is anatomical: Michael De Bellis at the University of Pittsburgh Medical Center used magnetic resonance imaging to compare the hippocampi of subjects 14 to 21 years old who abused alcohol to the hippocampi of those who did not. He found that the longer and the more a young person had been drinking, the smaller his hippocampus. The average size difference between healthy teens and alcohol abusers was roughly 10 percent. That is a lot of brain cells.

15. De Bellis speculates that the shrinkage may be due to cell damage and death that occurs during withdrawal from alcohol. Withdrawal is the brain's way of trying to get back to normal after prolonged or heavy drinking. It can leave the hands jittery, set off the

classic headache, generate intense anxiety, and even provoke seizures, as neurons that had adjusted to the presence of alcohol try to adjust to its absence. Because alcohol slows down the transmission of nerve signals—in part by stopping glutamate from activating its NDMA receptors—nerve cells under the influence react by increasing the number and sensitivity of these receptors. When drinking stops, the brain is suddenly stuck with too many hyperactive receptors.

16. Mark Prendergast, a neuroscientist at the University of Kentucky, recently revealed one way these hyperactive receptors kill brain cells. First, he exposed rat hippocampal slices to alcohol for 10 days, then removed the alcohol. Following withdrawal, he stained the tissue with a fluorescent dye that lit up dead and dying cells. When exposed to an alcohol concentration of about .08 percent, cell death increased some 25 percent above the baseline. When concentrations were two or three times higher, he wrote in a recent issue of *Alcoholism: Clinical and Experimental Research*, the number of dead cells shot up to 100 percent above the baseline.

17. Prendergast says that the younger brain tissue was far more sensitive. Preadolescent tissue suffered four to five times more cell death than did adult tissue. In all cases, most of the death occurred in hippocampal cells that were packed with NMDA receptors. To home in on the cause, he treated another batch of brain slices with the drug MK-801, which blocks NMDA receptors. He reasoned that if overexcitability during alcohol withdrawal was causing cell death, blocking the receptors should minimize the carnage. It did, by about 75 percent.

18. Now Prendergast is examining what makes the receptors so lethal. By tracking radioactive calcium, he found that the overexcited receptors open floodgates that allow calcium to swamp the cell. Too much calcium can turn on suicide genes that cause the neuron to break down its own membrane. Indeed, that is exactly what Prendergast observed during alcohol withdrawal: Overactive receptors opened wide, and the influx of calcium became a raging flood.

19. Prendergast says that four or five drinks may cause a mild withdrawal. And, according to Harvard's Wechsler, 44 percent of college students binge in this manner. More alarming, 23 percent of them consume 72 percent of all the alcohol that college students drink.

20. *Chuck was 15 the first time he binged on warm beers chugged with friends late at night in a vacant house. Six years later, celebrating his 21st birthday, he rapidly downed four shots of vodka in his dorm room. Then he and his friends drove through the snowy night to a sorority party at a bar, where he consumed another 16 drinks. Chuck's friends later told him how the rest of the night unfolded. He danced in a cage. He spun on the floor. He careened around the parking lot with a friend on his back. Halfway home, he stumbled out of the car and threw up. A friend half carried him home down frozen roads at 2 a.m. "I don't remember any of this," Chuck says. But he does*

remember the hangover he lived with for two days, as his brain and body withdrew from the booze.

21. Recent human studies support a conclusion Prendergast drew from his molecular experiments: The greatest brain damage from alcohol occurs during withdrawal. At the University of California at San Diego and the VA San Diego Health Care System, Sandra Brown, Susan Tapert, and Gregory Brown have been following alcohol-dependent adolescents for eight years. Repeated testing shows that problem drinkers perform more poorly on tests of cognition and learning than do nondrinkers. Furthermore, "the single best predictor of neuropsychological deficits for adolescents is withdrawal symptoms," says principal investigator Sandra Brown.

22. The psychologists recruited a group of 33 teenagers aged 15 and 16, all heavy drinkers. On average, each teen had used alcohol more than 750 times–the equivalent of drinking every day for two and a half years. Bingeing was common. The teens downed an average of eight drinks at each sitting. The researchers matched drinkers with nondrinkers of the same gender and similar age, IQ, socioeconomic background, and family history of alcohol use. Then, three weeks after the drinkers had their last drink, all the teens took a two-hour battery of tests.

23. The teens with alcohol problems had a harder time recalling information, both verbal and nonverbal, that they had learned 20 minutes earlier. Words such as *apple* and *football* escaped them. The performance difference was about 10 percent. "It's not serious brain damage, but it's the difference of a grade, a pass or a fail," Tapert says. Other tests evaluated skills needed for map learning, geometry, or science. Again, there was a 10 percent difference in performance.

24. "The study shows that just several years of heavy alcohol use by youth can adversely affect their brain functions in ways that are critical to learning," Sandra Brown says. She is following the group of teenagers until they reach age 30, and some have already passed 21. "Those who continue to use alcohol heavily are developing attentional deficits in addition to the memory and problem-solving deficits that showed up early on," Brown says. "In the past we thought of alcohol as a more benign drug. It's not included in the war on drugs. This study clearly demonstrates that the most popular drug is also an incredibly dangerous drug."

25. Brown's research team is also using functional magnetic resonance imaging to compare the brain function of alcohol abusers and nondrinkers. Initial results show that brains of young adults with a history of alcohol dependence are less active than the brains of nondrinkers during tasks that require spatial working memory (comparable to the maze task that White conducted on rats). In addition, the adolescent drinkers seem to exhibit greater levels of brain activity when they are exposed to alcohol related stimuli. For instance, when the drinkers read words such as *wasted* or *tequila* on a screen, the nucleus accumbens–a small section of the brain associated with craving–lights up.

26. The nucleus accumbens is integral to the brain's so-called pleasure circuit, which scientists now believe undergoes major remodeling during adolescence. Underlying the pleasure circuit is the neurotransmitter dopamine. Sex, food, and many drugs, including alcohol, can all induce the release of dopamine, which creates feelings of pleasure and in turn encourages repetition of the original behavior. During adolescence, the balance of dopamine activity temporarily shifts away from the nucleus accumbens, the brain's key pleasure and reward center, to the prefrontal cortex. Linda Spear, a developmental psychobiologist at Binghamton University in New York, speculates that as a result of this shift in balance, teenagers may find drugs less rewarding than earlier or later in life. And if the drugs produce less of a kick, more will be needed for the same effect. "In the case of alcohol, this may lead to binge drinking," she says.

27. *When Lynn was a freshman in high school, she liked to hang out at her friend John's apartment. More often than not, his father would be drinking beer. "He was like, 'Help yourself,' " Lynn says. Friends would come over and play drinking games until four or five in the morning. The longer the games continued, the tougher the rules became, doubling and tripling the number of drinks consumed. One night, Lynn came home drunk. Her mother talked her through her options, sharing stories of relatives who had ruined their lives drinking. Lynn struggled with her choices. A year later she still drinks, but she's kept a pact with her girlfriends to stop bingeing.*

28. During adolescence, the prefrontal cortex changes more than any other part of the brain. At around age 11 or 12, its neurons branch out like crazy, only to be seriously pruned back in the years that follow. All this tumult is to good purpose. In the adult brain, the prefrontal cortex executes the thought processes adolescents struggle to master: the ability to plan ahead, think abstractly, and integrate information to make sound decisions.

29. Now there is evidence that the prefrontal cortex and associated areas are among those most damaged in the brains of bingeing adolescents. Fulton Crews, director of the Center for Alcohol Studies at the University of North Carolina at Chapel Hill, has studied the patterns of cell death in the brains of adolescent and adult rats after four-day drinking bouts. While both groups showed damage in the back areas of the brain and in the frontally located olfactory bulb, used for smell, only the adolescents suffered brain damage in other frontal areas.

30. That youthful damage was severe. It extended from the rat's olfactory bulb to the interconnected parts of the brain that process sensory information and memories to make associations, such as "This smell and the sight of that wall tell me I'm in a place where I previously faced down an enemy." The regions of cell death in the rat experiment corresponded to the human prefrontal cortex and to parts of the limbic system.

31. The limbic system, which includes the hippocampus, changes throughout adolescence, according to recent work by Jay Giedd at the National Institute of Mental Health in Bethesda, Maryland. The limbic

system not only encodes memory but is also mobilized when a person is hungry or frightened or angry; it helps the brain process survival impulses. The limbic system and the prefrontal cortex must work in concert for a person to make sound decisions.

32. Damage to the prefrontal cortex and the limbic system is especially worrisome because they play an important role in the formation of an adult personality. "Binge drinking could be making permanent long-term changes in the final neural physiology, which is expressed as personality and behavior in the individual," Crews says. But he readily acknowledges that such conclusions are hypothetical. "It's very hard to prove this stuff. You can't do an experiment in which you change people's brains."

33. Nonetheless, evidence of the vulnerability of young people to alcohol is mounting. A study by Bridget Grant of the National Institute on Alcohol Abuse and Alcoholism shows that the younger someone is when he begins to regularly drink alcohol, the more likely that individual will eventually become an alcoholic. Grant found that 40 percent of the drinkers who got started before age 15 were classified later in life as alcohol dependent, compared with only 10 percent of those who began drinking at age 21 or 22. Overall, beginning at age 15, the risk of future alcohol dependence decreased by 14 percent with each passing year of abstention.

34. The study leaves unanswered whether early regular drinking is merely a marker of later abuse or whether it results in long-term changes in the brain that increase the later propensity for abuse. "It's got to be both," Crews says. For one thing, he points out that studies of rats and people have shown that repeated alcohol use makes it harder for a person—or a rat—to learn new ways of doing things, rather than repeating the same actions over and over again. In short, the way alcohol changes the brain makes it increasingly difficult over time to stop reaching for beer after beer after beer.

35. Ultimately, the collateral damage caused by having so many American adolescents reach for one drink after another may be incalculable. "People in their late teens have been drinking heavily for generations. We're not a society of idiots, but we're not a society of Einsteins either," says Swartzwelder. "What if you've compromised your function by 7 percent or 10 percent and never known the difference?" ⌘

Getting Stupid
by Bernice Wuethrich

1. *Sarah, a high school senior, drinks in moderation, but many of her friends do not. At one party, a classmate passed out after downing more than 20 shots of hard liquor and had to be rushed to a local emergency room. At another party a friend got sick, so Sarah made her drink water, dressed her in a sweatshirt to keep her warm, and lay her in bed, with a bucket on the floor. Then she brushed the girl's long hair away from her face so that it wouldn't get coated with vomit. "Every weekend, drinking is the only thing people do. Every single party has alcohol," says Sarah. (The names of the teenagers in these stories have been changed to protect their privacy.)*

ST passing out, alcohol poisoning

ST vomiting, choking hazard

2. The most recent statistics from the U.S. Substance Abuse and Mental Health Services Administration's National Household Survey on Drug Abuse indicate that nearly 7 million youths between the ages of 12 and 20 binge-drink at least once a month. And despite the fact that many colleges have cracked down on drinking, Henry Wechsler of the Harvard School of Public Health says that two of every five college students still binge-drink regularly. For a male that means downing five or more drinks in a row; for a female it means consuming four drinks in one session at least once in a two-week period.

3. Few teens seem to worry much about what such drinking does to their bodies. Cirrhosis of the liver is unlikely to catch up with them for decades, and heart disease must seem as remote as retirement. But new research suggests that young drinkers are courting danger. Because their brains are still developing well into their twenties, teens who drink excessively may be destroying significant amounts of mental capacity in ways that are more dramatic than in older drinkers.

LT physical—cirrhosis, heart disease

LT psychological—brain damage

4. Scientists have long known that excessive alcohol consumption among adults over long periods of time can create brain damage, ranging from a mild loss of motor skills to psychosis and even the inability to form memories. But less has been known about the impact alcohol has on youger brains. Until recently, scientists assumed that a youthful brain is more resilient than an adult brain and could escape many of the worst ills of alcohol. But some researchers are now beginning to question this assumption. Preliminary results from several studies indicate that the younger the brain is, the more it may be at risk. "The adolescent brain is a developing nervous system, and the things you do to it can change it," says Scott Swartzwelder, a neuropsychologist at Duke University and the U.S. Department of Veterans Affairs.

ST motor skills
LT psych—psychosis, memory loss

5. Teen drinkers appear to be most susceptible to damage in the hippocampus, a structure buried deep in the brain that is responsible for many types of learning and memory, and the prefrontal cortex, located behind the forehead, which is the brain's chief decision maker and voice of reason. Both areas, especially the prefrontal cortex, undergo dramatic change in the second decade of life.

LT psych—damage to hippocampus, prefrontal cortex; learning, memory, decision-making, reasoning

6. Swartzwelder and his team have been studying how alcohol affects the hippocampus, an evolutionarily old part of the brain that is similar in rats and humans. Six years ago, when Swartzwelder published his first paper suggesting that alcohol disrupts the hippocampus more severely in adolescent rats than in adult rats, "people didn't believe it," he says. Since then, his research has shown that the adolescent brain is more easily damaged in the structures that regulate the acquisition and storage of memories.

LT psych—memory

7. Learning depends on communication between nerve cells, or neurons, within the hippocampus. To communicate, a neuron fires an electrical signal down its axon, a single fiber extending away from the cell's center. In response, the axon releases chemical messengers, called neurotransmitters, which bind to receptors on the receiving branches of neighboring cells. Depending on the types of neurotransmitters released, the receiving cell may be jolted into action or settle more deeply into rest.

8. But the formation of memories requires more than the simple firing or inhibition of nerve cells. There must be some physical change in the hippocampal neurons that represents the encoding of new information. Scientists believe that this change occurs in the synapses, the tiny gaps between neurons that neurotransmitters traverse. Repeated use of synapses seems to increase their ability to fire up connecting cells. Laboratory experiments on brain tissue can induce this process, called long-term potentiation. Researchers assume that something similar takes place in the intact living brain, although it is impossible to observe directly. Essentially, if the repetitive neural reverberations are strong enough, they burn in new patterns of synaptic circuitry to encode memory, just as the more often a child recites his ABCs, the better he knows them.

9. Swartzwelder's first clue that alcohol powerfully disrupts memory in the adolescent brain came from studying rat hippocampi. He found that alcohol blocks long-term potentiation in adolescent brain tissue much more than in adult tissue. Next, Swartzwelder identified a likely explanation. Long-term potentiation—and thus memory formation—relies in large part on the action of a neurotransmitter known as glutamate, the brain's chemical kingpin of neural excitation. Glutamate strengthens a cell's electrical stimulation when it binds to a docking port called the NMDA receptor. If the receptor is blocked, so is long-term potentiation, and thus memory formation. Swartzwelder found that exposure to the equivalent of just two beers inhibits the NMDA receptors in the hippocampal cells of adolescent rats, while more than twice as much is required to produce the same effect in adult rats. These findings led him to suspect that alcohol consumption might have a dramatic impact on the ability of adolescents to learn. So he set up a series of behavioral tests.

LT psych—memory formation, ability to learn

10. First, Swartzwelder's team dosed adolescent and adult rats with alcohol and ran them through maze-learning tests. Compared with the adult rats, the adolescents failed miserably. To see whether similar results held true for humans, Swartzwelder recruited a group of volunteers aged 21 to 29 years old. He couldn't use younger subjects because of laws that forbid drinking before age 21. He chose to split

the volunteers into two groups: 21 to 24 years old and 25 to 29 years old. "While I wouldn't argue that these younger folks are adolescents, even in their early twenties their brains are still developing," Swartzwelder says. After three drinks, with a blood-alcohol level slightly below the National Highway Traffic Safety Administration's recommended limit–.08 percent–the younger group's learning was impaired 25 percent more than the older group's.

LT psych—learning impairment

11. Intrigued by these results, Swartzwelder's colleague Aaron White, a biological psychologist at Duke, set out to discover how vulnerable the adolescent brain is to long-term damage. He gave adolescent and adult rats large doses of alcohol every other day for 20 days–the equivalent of a 150-pound human chugging 24 drinks in a row. Twenty days after the last binge, when the adolescent rats had reached adulthood, White trained them in a maze-memory task roughly akin to that performed by a human when remembering the location of his car in a parking garage.

12. Both the younger and older rats performed equally well when sober. But when intoxicated, those who had binged as adolescents performed much worse. "Binge alcohol exposure in adolescence appears to produce long-lasting changes in brain function," White says. He suspects that early damage caused by alcohol could surface whenever the brain is taxed. He also suspects that the NMDA receptor is involved, because just as alcohol in the system inhibits the receptor, the drug's withdrawal overstimulates it– which can kill the cell outright.

LT psych—damage to memory functions

13. *During the fall semester last year, at least 11 college students died from alcohol related causes–at California State University at Chico, Colgate University in New York, Old Dominion University in Virginia, the University of Michigan, Vincennes University in Kentucky, Washington and Lee University in Virginia, and Washington State University. No one knows how many other students were rushed to emergency rooms for alcohol poisoning, but at Duke, 11 students had visited local ERs in just the first three weeks of school, and in only one night of partying, three students from the University of Tennessee were hospitalized.*

ST alcohol poisoning

LT phys—death

14. Students who drink heavily sometimes joke that they are killing a few brain cells. New research suggests that this is not funny. Some of the evidence is anatomical: Michael De Bellis at the University of Pittsburgh Medical Center used magnetic resonance imaging to compare the hippocampi of subjects 14 to 21 years old who abused alcohol to the hippocampi of those who did not. He found that the longer and the more a young person had been drinking, the smaller his hippocampus. The average size difference between healthy teens and alcohol abusers was roughly 10 percent. That is a lot of brain cells.

LT psych—shrinking hippocampus, loss of brain cells

715. De Bellis speculates that the shrinkage may be due to cell damage and death that occurs during withdrawal from alcohol. Withdrawal is the brain's way of trying to get back to normal after prolonged or heavy drinking. It can leave the hands jittery, set off the classic headache, generate intense anxiety, and even provoke

ST jitters, headache, anxiety, seizures

seizures, as neurons that had adjusted to the presence of alcohol try to adjust to its absence. Because alcohol slows down the transmission of nerve signals—in part by stopping glutamate from activating its NDMA receptors—nerve cells under the influence react by increasing the number and sensitivity of these receptors. When drinking stops, the brain is suddenly stuck with too many hyperactive receptors.

16. Mark Prendergast, a neuroscientist at the University of Kentucky, recently revealed one way these hyperactive receptors kill brain cells. First, he exposed rat hippocampal slices to alcohol for 10 days, then removed the alcohol. Following withdrawal, he stained the tissue with a fluorescent dye that lit up dead and dying cells. When exposed to an alcohol concentration of about .08 percent, cell death increased some 25 percent above the baseline. When concentrations were two or three times higher, he wrote in a recent issue of *Alcoholism: Clinical and Experimental Research*, the number of dead cells shot up to 100 percent above the baseline.

LT psych—brain cell death

17. Prendergast says that the younger brain tissue was far more sensitive. Preadolescent tissue suffered four to five times more cell death than did adult tissue. In all cases, most of the death occurred in hippocampal cells that were packed with NMDA receptors. To home in on the cause, he treated another batch of brain slices with the drug MK-801, which blocks NMDA receptors. He reasoned that if overexcitability during alcohol withdrawal was causing cell death, blocking the receptors should minimize the carnage. It did, by about 75 percent.

18. Now Prendergast is examining what makes the receptors so lethal. By tracking radioactive calcium, he found that the overexcited receptors open floodgates that allow calcium to swamp the cell. Too much calcium can turn on suicide genes that cause the neuron to break down its own membrane. Indeed, that is exactly what Prendergast observed during alcohol withdrawal: Overactive receptors opened wide, and the influx of calcium became a raging flood.

19. Prendergast says that four or five drinks may cause a mild withdrawal. And, according to Harvard's Wechsler, 44 percent of college students binge in this manner. More alarming, 23 percent of them consume 72 percent of all the alcohol that college students drink.

20. *Chuck was 15 the first time he binged on warm beers chugged with friends late at night in a vacant house. Six years later, celebrating his 21st birthday, he rapidly downed four shots of vodka in his dorm room. Then he and his friends drove through the snowy night to a sorority party at a bar, where he consumed another 16 drinks. Chuck's friends later told him how the rest of the night unfolded. He danced in a cage. He spun on the floor. He careened around the parking lot with a friend on his back. Halfway home, he stumbled out of the car and threw up. A friend half carried him home down frozen roads at 2 a.m. "I don't remember any of this," Chuck says. But he does remember the hangover he lived with for two days, as his brain and body withdrew from the booze.*

ST bizarre behavior, vomiting, memory loss, hangover

21. Recent human studies support a conclusion Prendergast drew from his molecular experiments: The greatest brain damage from alcohol occurs during withdrawal. At the University of California at San Diego and the VA San Diego Health Care System, Sandra Brown, Susan Tapert, and Gregory Brown have been following alcohol-dependent adolescents for eight years. Repeated testing shows that problem drinkers perform more poorly on tests of cognition and learning than do nondrinkers. Furthermore, "the single best predictor of neuropsychological deficits for adolescents is withdrawal symptoms," says principal investigator Sandra Brown.

LT psych—poor performance on tests of cognition, learning

22. The psychologists recruited a group of 33 teenagers aged 15 and 16, all heavy drinkers. On average, each teen had used alcohol more than 750 times–the equivalent of drinking every day for two and a half years. Bingeing was common. The teens downed an average of eight drinks at each sitting. The researchers matched drinkers with nondrinkers of the same gender and similar age, IQ, socioeconomic background, and family history of alcohol use. Then, three weeks after the drinkers had their last drink, all the teens took a two-hour battery of tests.

23. The teens with alcohol problems had a harder time recalling information, both verbal and nonverbal, that they had learned 20 minutes earlier. Words such as *apple* and *football* escaped them. The performance difference was about 10 percent. "It's not serious brain damage, but it's the difference of a grade, a pass or a fail," Tapert says. Other tests evaluated skills needed for map learning, geometry, or science. Again, there was a 10 percent difference in performance.

LT psych—recall, skills for map reading, geometry, science

24. "The study shows that just several years of heavy alcohol use by youth can adversely affect their brain functions in ways that are critical to learning," Sandra Brown says. She is following the group of teenagers until they reach age 30, and some have already passed 21. "Those who continue to use alcohol heavily are developing attentional deficits in addition to the memory and problem-solving deficits that showed up early on," Brown says. "In the past we thought of alcohol as a more benign drug. It's not included in the war on drugs. This study clearly demonstrates that the most popular drug is also an incredibly dangerous drug."

LT psych—attention deficits; memory and problem-solving deficits

25. Brown's research team is also using functional magnetic resonance imaging to compare the brain function of alcohol abusers and nondrinkers. Initial results show that brains of young adults with a history of alcohol dependence are less active than the brains of nondrinkers during tasks that require spatial working memory (comparable to the maze task that White conducted on rats). In addition, the adolescent drinkers seem to exhibit greater levels of brain activity when they are exposed to alcohol related stimuli. For instance, when the drinkers read words such as *wasted* or *tequila* on a screen, the nucleus accumbens–a small section of the brain associated with craving–lights up.

LT psych—reduced brain activity, increased craving after stimuli

26. The nucleus accumbens is integral to the brain's so-called pleasure circuit, which scientists now believe undergoes major remodeling during adolescence. Underlying the pleasure circuit is the neurotransmitter dopamine. Sex, food, and many drugs, including alcohol, can all induce the release of dopamine, which creates feelings of pleasure and in turn encourages repetition of the original behavior. During adolescence, the balance of dopamine activity temporarily shifts away from the nucleus accumbens, the brain's key pleasure and reward center, to the prefrontal cortex. Linda Spear, a developmental psychobiologist at Binghamton University in New York, speculates that as a result of this shift in balance, teenagers may find drugs less rewarding than earlier or later in life. And if the drugs produce less of a kick, more will be needed for the same effect. "In the case of alcohol, this may lead to binge drinking," she says.

LT psych—need for increased amounts of alcohol to cause pleasure

27. *When Lynn was a freshman in high school, she liked to hang out at her friend John's apartment. More often than not, his father would be drinking beer. "He was like, 'Help yourself,' " Lynn says. Friends would come over and play drinking games until four or five in the morning. The longer the games continued, the tougher the rules became, doubling and tripling the number of drinks consumed. One night, Lynn came home drunk. Her mother talked her through her options, sharing stories of relatives who had ruined their lives drinking. Lynn struggled with her choices. A year later she still drinks, but she's kept a pact with her girlfriends to stop bingeing.*

28. During adolescence, the prefrontal cortex changes more than any other part of the brain. At around age 11 or 12, its neurons branch out like crazy, only to be seriously pruned back in the years that follow. All this tumult is to good purpose. In the adult brain, the prefrontal cortex executes the thought processes adolescents struggle to master: the ability to plan ahead, think abstractly, and integrate information to make sound decisions.

LT psych—damage to prefrontal cortex; planning, abstract thinking, integration of information

29. Now there is evidence that the prefrontal cortex and associated areas are among those most damaged in the brains of bingeing adolescents. Fulton Crews, director of the Center for Alcohol Studies at the University of North Carolina at Chapel Hill, has studied the patterns of cell death in the brains of adolescent and adult rats after four-day drinking bouts. While both groups showed damage in the back areas of the brain and in the frontally located olfactory bulb, used for smell, only the adolescents suffered brain damage in other frontal areas.

30. That youthful damage was severe. It extended from the rat's olfactory bulb to the interconnected parts of the brain that process sensory information and memories to make associations, such as "This smell and the sight of that wall tell me I'm in a place where I previously faced down an enemy." The regions of cell death in the rat experiment corresponded to the human prefrontal cortex and to parts of the limbic system.

LT psych—ability to process sensory information and memories, make associations

31. The limbic system, which includes the hippocampus, changes throughout adolescence, according to recent work by Jay Giedd at the National Institute of Mental Health in Bethesda, Maryland. The limbic

LT psych—damage to

system not only encodes memory but is also mobilized when a person is hungry or frightened or angry; it helps the brain process survival impulses. The limbic system and the prefrontal cortex must work in concert for a person to make sound decisions.

limbic system—memory, survival impulses, ability to make sound decisions

32. Damage to the prefrontal cortex and the limbic system is especially worrisome because they play an important role in the formation of an adult personality. "Binge drinking could be making permanent long-term changes in the final neural physiology, which is expressed as personality and behavior in the individual," Crews says. But he readily acknowledges that such conclusions are hypothetical. "It's very hard to prove this stuff. You can't do an experiment in which you change people's brains."

LT psych—permanent damage to neural physiology; changes in personality, behavior

33. Nonetheless, evidence of the vulnerability of young people to alcohol is mounting. A study by Bridget Grant of the National Institute on Alcohol Abuse and Alcoholism shows that the younger someone is when he begins to regularly drink alcohol, the more likely that individual will eventually become an alcoholic. Grant found that 40 percent of the drinkers who got started before age 15 were classified later in life as alcohol dependent, compared with only 10 percent of those who began drinking at age 21 or 22. Overall, beginning at age 15, the risk of future alcohol dependence decreased by 14 percent with each passing year of abstention.

LT psych—danger of alcoholism

34. The study leaves unanswered whether early regular drinking is merely a marker of later abuse or whether it results in long-term changes in the brain that increase the later propensity for abuse. "It's got to be both," Crews says. For one thing, he points out that studies of rats and people have shown that repeated alcohol use makes it harder for a person—or a rat—to learn new ways of doing things, rather than repeating the same actions over and over again. In short, the way alcohol changes the brain makes it increasingly difficult over time to stop reaching for beer after beer after beer.

LT psych—difficulty learning new ways of doing things

35. Ultimately, the collateral damage caused by having so many American adolescents reach for one drink after another may be incalculable. "People in their late teens have been drinking heavily for generations. We're not a society of idiots, but we're not a society of Einsteins either," says Swartzwelder. "What if you've compromised your function by 7 percent or 10 percent and never known the difference?" ⌘

Chapter 11

Using Relevant Material

This chapter provides some examples to help you learn how to pick out the information you want from the books, magazines, Web sites, and other sources that you find. You'll need to sharpen this skill **before** you actually start filling your note cards with writing.

Step 1. To find relevant passages, you will need to learn to skim, that is, to read rapidly, looking for facts, ideas, quotations, statistics, or examples to support your major topics. Although sometimes you will have to study a passage carefully, it is not always necessary to read every word when you are looking for useful information. When possible, use the table of contents and index to help locate key passages.

Step 2. With your thesis statement and topic headings in mind, zero in on passages you can use. Take down key information word-for-word, ignoring the rest. **Copy only what is relevant.**

Example 1.
Here is how Dan managed this step. He was doing research on the jazz singer Billie Holiday for an oral presentation in which he planned to tell something about her life and career, and to play some tapes of her singing. His topic headings were **Early Life**, **Career**, and **Personality**. He looked at her autobiography, where she devotes several chapters to her childhood. Dan was looking for an incident that would be typical of the hardships she endured. Of the many possibilities, he finally chose one. The note card he prepared looked like this:

> *Childhood and Early Life*   Holiday 6-7
>
> *All of us were crowded in that little house like fishes. I had to sleep in the same bed with Henry and Elsie, and Henry used to wet it every night. It made (7) me mad and sometimes I'd get up and sit in a chair until morning. Then my cousin Ida would come in the morning, see the bed, accuse me of wetting it, and start beating me. When she was upset she'd beat me something awful. Not with a strap, not with a spank on the ass, but with her fist or a whip.*

When Dan wrote his rough draft, he used the information on the card in the paragraph below. Notice that he has thoroughly paraphrased the material, using only a brief direct quotation, and he has documented it accurately. He has also added his own observation to the paragraph by speculating about the effect of this early violence on Holiday's personality.

After her father went on the road with the musical group, McKinney's Cotton Pickers, Holiday's mother sent her to live with her grandparents and a number of other relatives. The house was small, and living conditions were difficult. Holiday had to share a bed with her Aunt Ida's two small children, one of whom usually wet the bed. Her aunt blamed Holiday, even though she was not guilty, and her aunt frequently beat her "with her fists or a whip" (Holiday 6-7). The abuse she suffered as a child undoubtedly left a mark on Holiday, who never stopped hating Aunt Ida. She was later prone to use violence herself, probably a consequence of experiencing violence as a child. But she also learned to be a survivor, a skill she needed throughout her trouble-filled life.

Example 2.

Sarah is writing about the importance of symbolism in <u>The Adventures of Huckleberry Finn</u>. Under the topic heading **The River**, she recorded on Card 1 the following passage from T. S. Eliot's introduction to that novel:

The River   Eliot 325

It is the River that controls the voyage of Huck and Jim; that will not let them land at Cairo, where Jim could have reached freedom; it is the River that separates them and deposits Huck for a time in the Grangerford household; the River re-unites them, and then compels upon them the unwelcome company of the King and the Duke. Recurrently we are reminded of its presence and its power.

Card 1

Later, Sarah found some relevant information in Leo Marx's essay "Mr. Eliot, Mr. Trilling, and <u>Huckleberry Finn</u>." Her word-for-word notes, under the same topic heading **The River** but on Card 2, look like this:

The River   Marx 334

Then there is the river; after each adventure Huck and Jim return to the raft and the river. Both Mr. Trilling and Mr. Eliot speak eloquently of the river as a source of unity, and they refer to the river as a god. . . . It is a source of food and beauty and terror and serenity of mind. But above all, it provides motion; it is the means by which Huck and Jim move away from a menacing civilization.

Card 2

In her rough draft, Sarah wrote the following paragraph to introduce her discussion of the various levels of symbolic meaning that critics have attributed to the river. Notice that she has thoroughly paraphrased the borrowed material, and she has documented it correctly.[*]

Many critics have recognized the river as a major symbol in <u>Huck Finn</u>, and they have suggested many different interpretations. But whatever its symbolic value, the river plays a crucial role in the narrative. It determines the action, taking Huck and Jim past Cairo and preventing Jim's escape up the Ohio River. The Mississippi River separates them, and it brings them together again. It brings them adventures, both joyful and terrifying (Eliot 325).

Although some incidents take place away from the river, the most important action—especially Huck's decisions and discoveries—all occur on the raft. The river sustains them on their journey, providing fish and occasional salvage. It brings them, briefly at least, a peaceful, idyllic existence, and its current carries them "away from a menacing civilization" (Marx 334). Ironically, it takes them farther into the deep South, where Jim's quest for freedom will be even more difficult.

---

[*] Both the articles cited are in Samuel L. Clemens, <u>The Adventures of Huckleberry Finn</u>, Norton Critical Editions (New York: Norton, 1962). The Billie Holiday example is based on Billie Holiday, <u>Lady Sings the Blues</u> (New York: Avon, 1976).

Summary

Using Relevant Material

To find useful information for your note cards:

- Skim documents for relevant passages.

- Copy word-for-word onto note cards information that supports your thesis statement and major topics.

- Head each note card with the appropriate topic heading, using subtopics.

- In the rough draft, paraphrase thoroughly and use brief direct quotations from your note card material. Document as you write.

Sample Note Card

Topic heading	Labyrinths in Churches
Author's name	
Page	Doob 117

England had turf-mazes and other northern countries had stone labyrinths to familiarize their inhabitants with the characteristic form of the unicursal maze (and perhaps with some aspects of the labyrinth as metaphor), but northern France and northern Italy located their diagrammatic mazes in churches and cathedrals.

Borrowed material quoted word-for-word

Chapter 12
Taking Notes

Although there are other methods of note taking for a research paper, this chapter will focus on the one that many writers and most teachers prefer—the note card method for recording the information that you find, hereafter referred to as <u>borrowed material</u>. This method provides a convenient way to organize and retrieve information; to teach selectivity in note taking; to avoid plagiarism; and to check the accuracy of information in the final product.

A laptop computer can make note taking a lot easier, but not everyone has one, so we'll describe the widely used note card procedure. Although using a photocopying machine can also be helpful, it doesn't do the job of **selecting relevant material and placing it under the right heading,** so it can't replace note cards. But the copier is useful for reproducing charts, graphs, and diagrams, and for making copies of long or difficult articles that you may need to study carefully and then to underline, highlight, or annotate before you start taking notes. If your teacher wants you to use a different method of note taking, instead of the one described below, then he or she will give you special instructions. There are a number of electronic alternatives to note cards, but again, they are not always available to all students throughout the research process.

Refer to the sample note card on the preceding page as you read through the steps in the note taking process.

Steps in note taking

Step I.   **Use 4x6 or 5x8 index cards, NOT 3x5s**, which are too small. You will need 20 to 25 for a five-page paper.

         On an additional card, write your revised **thesis statement** and list your three or more **major supporting topics.** Keep these constantly in mind as you take notes so that you will not waste time copying useless material.

         Use a pen and write legibly.

Step 2.   Head each card with a **topic heading** that identifies the subject matter on the card. Remember that these topics correspond to the supporting topics in your working outline. Some typical topic headings might be:

         Problem-Solving Ability, for a paper on dolphin intelligence.

Damage to Hemlock Forests, for a paper on the effects of acid rain.

Color Symbolism, for a paper on symbolism in James Joyce's <u>Portrait of the Artist as a Young Man</u>.

Have no more than three or four major topic headings. If you seem to have more topics, consider treating them as **subheadings** under your **major topic headings**. For example, under the major topic heading **Problem-Solving Ability**, you might use the subheadings **Locating hidden objects, Negotiating a maze,** and **Avoiding danger.** Under the major topic heading **Color Symbolism**, you might use **Red, Green,** and **Black** as subheadings. Under **Damage to Hemlock Forests,** your cards might include subheadings that list specific kinds of damage.

Hint: You might head a few cards **Miscellaneous**, or **General Information**, for items that do not fit into specific categories but might prove useful somewhere.

Step 3. In the upper right corner of each card, write the author's last name and the page where you find the information. You can abbreviate the name because you have recorded complete publication information for all your sources on your source cards. If there is no author, as in an unsigned editorial or newspaper article, use the first important word of the title.

Examples:

On your **source card** (3x5), you wrote Doob, Penelope Reed. <u>The Idea of the Labyrinth from Classical Antiquity through the Middle Ages</u>. Ithaca: Cornell UP, 1990.

On your **note card** (4x6), write only Doob 117 in the upper right corner—the author's last name and the page where you found useful information. Then write the information found on page 117 that you plan to use in your paper, copying it accurately onto your card.

If you also have a source card for Doob's book <u>Nebuchadnezzar's Children: Conventions of Madness in Middle English Literature</u>, then add Idea to the card using the first book (Doob Idea), and Nebuchadnezzar to cards with information from the second (Doob Nebuchadnezzar).

Step 4. **Put only one idea or entry from one source on each card.** This may include several sentences, but they should be continuous and should relate to the same subject. The information that you put on a particular card might be:

- The writer's description of a childhood incident.
- A critic's interpretation of a symbol in a poem.
- A stage in a natural process.
- A historian's account of the reasons for Tecumseh's defeat at Maguaga.

You may write on both sides of each card, and you may continue an entry, if necessary, onto another card. Repeat author and page information on the second card, e.g., Doob 118, Doob 124. If quoted material occurs on consecutive pages, insert the new page number on the card, as in the model on page 88.

Step 5. **Use Direct Quotes Only**—no paraphrases, no summaries.

Omit what is not immediately pertinent to the topic. Use care in choosing material to quote; do not just copy everything in sight. Use three spaced dots . . . (ellipsis points) to show omissions. If the author you are quoting uses ellipsis points, then you may add your own ellipses and place them inside square brackets to show that the omission is not in the original text. Use square brackets also to insert words needed for clarity: "[Marquez's] luminous narrative . . . rivals the most remarkable stories of man's struggles against the sea."

Do not put quotation marks around the whole entry on the card because **EVERYTHING** on your note cards is word-for-word, verbatim, an exact copy of the original. You will use **paraphrasing** and **summarizing** in your paper, but your note cards should contain only material that is identical to the original, some of which you may later use as **direct quotations**.

Note:
Step 5 is critical in preventing plagiarism.

A few more hints:

- You may want to mark information that you think is especially important, perhaps with an asterisk or by highlighting it.
- Where you have a comment or question of your own, you can add it right on the note card, placing it inside braces {. . .} to show that it is **your own observation** and is **not borrowed material**. This will help you remember to add your own comments later when you are writing your paper.
- Or you can use a different color ink or a special highlighter, say pink or blue, to mark your own comments and ideas, to distinguish them from your borrowed material.

Step 6. Check to make sure that the data you put on each card is relevant to the specific topic that is the heading of each card.

Examples:

- A baseball player's lifetime batting average does not belong on a note card headed **Childhood**.
- A comment on Dickens's writing style should not be on a card with the heading **Characterization**.
- Information about the koala's mating behavior does not belong on a card headed **Food Supply**.

Make sure that you copy accurately, including capitalization, spelling, and punctuation.

Step 7.   When you hand in your note cards for checking, add a top card with your name and class. Write your thesis statement in its present form and your three or four major topics on the card, and put a rubber band around the stack.

Or follow the specific instructions your teacher provides.

Sample Note Cards

Card 1 is a note card that Todd prepared during his research on symbolism in The Great Gatsby. He headed a second stack of cards **The Green Light**. A third pile had the topic heading **Dr. Eckleberg's Eyes**. On each set of cards he took down only information pertinent to that particular topic, in this case, the importance of different symbols in Fitzgerald's novel.

Topic Heading ————

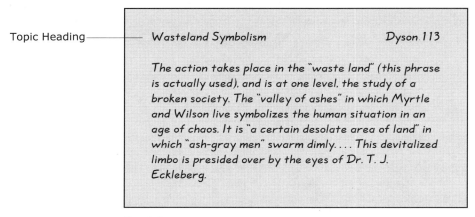

> *Wasteland Symbolism*   *Dyson 113*
>
> *The action takes place in the "waste land" (this phrase is actually used), and is at one level, the study of a broken society. The "valley of ashes" in which Myrtle and Wilson live symbolizes the human situation in an age of chaos. It is "a certain desolate area of land" in which "ash-gray men" swarm dimly.... This devitalized limbo is presided over by the eyes of Dr. T. J. Eckleberg.*

Card 1

Card 2 is from Melissa's paper on racism in professional tennis. She recorded information from Arthur Ashe's autobiography on several cards, and then consulted other books and articles on the history of tennis to learn about the experiences of other African-American athletes. Since her source cards include two different books by Ashe–Days of Grace and Off the Court–she identified each one on her note cards with the author's last name and the first important word of the title.

Topic Heading ——

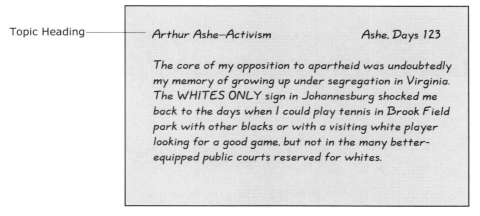

Card 2

Card 3 is part of Corey's research on the effects of insecticides. After looking at studies of DDT and other toxic substances, she split the topic into subtopics. Under the heading **long-term effects**, she recorded information about the insects' growing resistance to sprays, the increased mortality of birds that ate the insects, and the increased sterility of the birds that survived. Under **short-term effects,** she noted the immediate decrease of insects, reduction of typhus deaths, decrease in the spread of malaria, and the like.

Topic Heading ——

Sub Heading ——

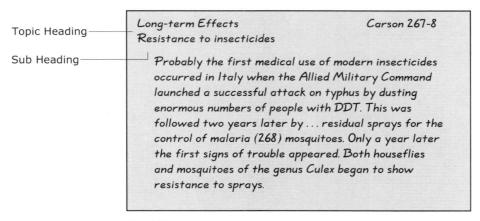

Card 3

Summary

Taking Notes

To prepare note cards:

- Take notes on 4x6 cards, in ink.

- Head each card with a Topic Heading; use subtopics if needed.

- Put the author's name and the page number in the upper right corner.

- Take only word-for-word, verbatim notes; no summary, no paraphrase.

- Put only one entry or idea from a given source on each card.

- Take down only information relevant to a specific topic.

- Jot down your own comments and ideas as you take notes, but keep them distinct from the borrowed material on the card.

Chapter 13
From Notes to Rough Draft

This chapter provides help for the next step—to begin drafting your paper. Your major task is integrating your borrowed material into your paper, keeping in mind that accuracy, honesty, smoothness, and the inclusion of your own ideas are all crucial.

A quick review of your recent steps shows that you have:

- Revised your thesis statement as you went along.
- Copied information accurately onto your note cards.
- Sorted your note cards into piles according to topic headings, discarding those that you can't use.
- Updated your topic outline by noting briefly the supporting information that you found under your major topics.

Warning: Some dead ends and traps to avoid:

- ☹ Plagiarism, usually by inadequate paraphrasing and faulty documentation.
- ☹ The necktie effect–endless stringing of quotations without adequate discussion.
- ☹ Careless copying or sloppy paraphrasing that may misrepresent the author's position.
- ☹ The "stick-it-to-'em" technique–putting in direct quotations without introductory phrases; the quotation stands alone like a lost soul at a party.

Step-by-step procedure for moving from notes to rough draft.

Steps for writing the rough draft

Step 1.   Replace your rough, tentative topic outline with an expanded topic outline and fill in the necessary information. A model of this outline is included in Appendix A. You will need a clear **topic sentence** to introduce each of the body sections of your paper. Note: We'll use the term **body sections** instead of **body paragraphs** since normally you will need several paragraphs to develop your ideas. Some books and some teachers call these **developmental paragraphs** and **developmental sections**.

Arrange your note cards for the first body section of your paper in the order you intend to use them, and number them in the upper left corner. Put aside those cards with information that does not support your topic sentence for this section. You may be able to use them elsewhere. Work on one section of your paper at a time.

Step 2.   Write the latest version of your **thesis statement** at the top of your paper and skip the next few lines.

Do not try to write your opening paragraph(s) now; leave that for later. More ideas will come to you as you write.

> **Be sure to double-space your rough draft.**
> It makes revision and editing much easier.

Step 3.   Write the **topic sentence** for your first body section, using your expanded topic outline and improving your topic sentence if you can. Make sure that this sentence introduces the main idea you plan to develop in the section. Use several additional sentences to make that idea clear.

Begin providing **support for that idea**, your first major topic, using the information from your cards in the order you have determined.

Remember that you will use borrowed material in three different ways: **paraphrase, summary, and direct quotation.** The next two chapters give a detailed explanation of these techniques.

Insert parenthetical citations (Levinson 47) **as you write**; do not even think about adding them later.

> **It's a cite-as-you-write process.**
> See Chapter 16A or Chapter 16B for details.

Step 4.   Remember that a direct quotation **always** requires a lead-in, that is, words and phrases to introduce it. Direct quotations are **never** rudely inserted without an introduction; they always follow such phrases as these:

> According to Senate Majority Leader Bill Frist (R-TN), "The Civil Rights Movement defined us as a nation . . ."

> As <u>Boston Globe</u> columnist Cathy Young points out, "Gulag revisionism is not stigmatized the way Holocaust revisionism is."

> Ezra Pound, one of the most famous and controversial poets of the twentieth century, observes, "Literature is language charged with meaning."

Keep the following rule in mind:

L-I .... lead in, using introductory words and phrases

Q .... quote accurately

F-U .... follow up with comments and explanation

Step 5. Continue importing the information from your note cards into your paper, introducing and citing as you go, until you have provided adequate support for this particular topic.

You must provide commentary and discussion of your borrowed material as well, but many students find it easier to get borrowed material from card to paper first and then to expand the discussion in the next step.

Step 6. Print out this section of your paper. The next steps require hard copy. Your draft will look like the first version of Meg's paper, which is on page 96.

With your note cards numbered in the order you used them, highlight the material from each one that appears in your paper. Put the number of the corresponding note card in the right margin of your paper. Your draft will now resemble the second version of Meg's paper, on page 97.

Step 7. Check your highlighted material, including your in-text citations, for accuracy, and make needed corrections.

Now go through your paper carefully, noting where you should add follow-up—comments, explanation, discussion, interpretation, and evaluation of borrowed material. Keep in mind that this is **your** paper and that you are presenting material to support a statement that **you** formulated and that **you** consider worth saying. Look at Meg's revised paragraph on page 98.

Step 8. Return to your first body section, and add the material you decide your first draft needs. Remember that without the addition of your own ideas, your paper will be a mere patchwork quilt of borrowed material instead of the excellent research paper that is your goal. Remember to review the comments and questions you jotted down on your cards as you were taking notes.

With each revision and rereading, see if you can make improvements in wording, sentence combining, and clarity. Provide transitions for smoothness and coherence.

Step 9. Repeat this process for the remaining body sections.

Keep all your material in a safe place, including source cards, outlines, note cards, and separate drafts of your paper. Paper clips, rubber bands, and large envelopes are also helpful. Remember that your teacher is unlikely to believe that your dog ate the whole enchilada.

Now let's follow a student through this process.

Meg's thesis statement is: To become a successful scientist, Marie Curie had to overcome many obstacles with hard work and determination. Meg's topic headings are **Childhood Influences**, **Major Professional Accomplishments**, and **Personal Qualities**. Her note cards about Curie's early life look like this:

Childhood, Youth   Smith 21

She was a timid child, small and nervous for her years
... She had a logical turn of mind, that might have
seemed a coldness to those who did not know her well.

Card 1

Childhood, Youth   Brown 223

Maria had intense powers of concentration and a
remarkable memory.

Card 2

```
Childhood, Youth                    Green 56


The immediate direction of Maria's future was decided
by money, or as was usual in her family, the lack of it ... .
Teaching, the family profession, would have to support
her.
```

Card 3

```
Childhood, Youth                    Jones 125


Most of all she was excited by physics and mathematics.
She had the concentration and persistence to take her
beyond the first flush of their novelty.
```

Card 4

The **first version** of Meg's paragraph looks like this:

Even when she was extremely young, Marie Curie showed the qualities that would later make her a world-renowned scientist. Growing up in Poland in the 1860s, she was a shy child who often kept to herself, trying to figure things out (Smith 21). Instead of playing games as other children did, she often spent time in reading and intellectual pursuits, in which, according to Robert Brown, she showed "intense powers of concentration and a remarkable memory" (223). She attended school for a while, but because her family was extremely poor, she was not able to continue. She decided to become a governess in order to support herself (Green 56). Later, following her sister, she went to Paris to attend the university. There, as Jones points out, "Most of all she was excited by physics and mathematics" (125). Showing the same ability to concentrate and keep working on a problem until she solved it, she soon distinguished herself and passed the difficult examination in physics (125). At 26, she had acquired an excellent scientific education.

On the preceding pages, you can see the exact copy of the borrowed material as it appears on Meg's note cards, and then, below it, you can see how that material came into her rough draft through direct quotation, paraphrase, and summary. The parenthetical citations provide the documentation, showing the exact source of each piece of information.

Notice that when the author's name occurs in the text, then only the page number occurs in the citation. Note also that subsequent references to other pages in the same work require only the page number, and not the author's name.

The **second version** of Meg's paragraph looks like this. Notice how she has highlighted all borrowed material and shown which card it came from. This makes it easy to see that the paragraph is almost entirely borrowed material, with no contributions from the author.

Even when she was extremely young, Marie Curie showed the qualities that would later make her a world-renowned scientist. Growing up in Poland in the 1860s, she was a shy child who often kept to herself, trying to figure things out (Smith 21). Instead of playing games as other children did, she often spent time in reading and intellectual pursuits, in which, according to Robert Brown, she showed "intense powers of concentration and a remarkable memory" (223). She attended school for a while, but because her family was extremely poor, she was not able to continue. She decided to become a governess in order to support herself (Green 56). Later, following her sister, she went to Paris to attend the university. There, as Jones points out, "Most of all she was excited by physics and mathematics" (125). Showing the same ability to concentrate and keep working on a problem until she solved it, she soon distinguished herself and passed the difficult examination in physics (125). At 26, she had acquired an excellent scientific education.

1

2

3

4

The paragraph below is Meg's **third version**. She has added supplementary material of her own, including comments, explanation, and discussion of the borrowed material. This new material is double underlined to help you see how to add your own interpretations, comments, and discussion. Without those additions, Meg's paragraph would be just wall-to-wall quoted material instead of a promising start for her essay.*

Even when she was extremely young, Marie Curie showed the qualities that would later make her a world-renowned scientist. Growing up in Poland in the 1860s, she was a shy child who often kept to herself, trying to figure things out (Smith 21). Instead of playing games as other children did, she often spent time in reading and intellectual pursuits, in which, according to Robert Brown, she showed "intense powers of concentration and a remarkable memory" (223). Although this helped prepare Curie for her future career, it probably did not make her popular with her classmates. Today she would be considered a "nerd." She attended school for a while, but because her family was extremely poor, she was not able to continue (Green 56). This must have been a terrible disappointment to her since school was the place where she excelled. But Curie did not spend much time feeling sorry for herself. She decided to become a governess in order to support herself (56). As soon as she could afford to, she followed her sister's example and went to Paris to attend the university. There, as Jones points out, "Most of all she was excited by physics and mathematics" (125). These were not fields that women tended to pursue, but apparently that did not bother her. Showing the same ability to concentrate and to keep working on a problem until she solved it, she soon distinguished herself and passed the difficult examination in physics (125). At 26, she had acquired an excellent scientific education and was ready to embark on the career that would eventually bring her the highest honors in science.

---

* The borrowed material in this example is adapted from Robert Reid, Marie Curie (New York: Signet, 1974).

Summary

From Notes to Rough Draft

To move from notes to rough draft:

- Turn your preliminary outline into an expanded topic outline, making each topic heading a topic sentence and filling in specific information under your major headings.

- Sort your note cards into piles under each major heading and number them in the order you will use them. Work on one section at a time.

- Support your topic sentence with information from your note cards, using paraphrase, summary, and direct quotation and providing all needed citations.

- Use lead-ins to introduce direct quotations and follow-ups to provide discussion of all borrowed material.

- Print out each section, highlighting and numbering borrowed material so that you can see where you need to add your own ideas and comments.

- Read over each section, revising and improving, adding and deleting. Then go on to the next section. Save all your materials—outlines, cards, printouts, copies, and drafts.

Chapter 14

Paraphrasing and Summarizing

In Chapter 13 we noted that one of the most difficult tasks students encounter when they move from note cards to rough draft is successfully incorporating borrowed material into their papers. This chapter provides some guidelines for paraphrasing and summarizing, and Chapter 15 covers techniques for using direct quotation.

Paraphrasing

You should paraphrase **most** of the borrowed material that you use in your paper. That means rewriting or restating another person's ideas **in your own words**. Keep in mind the following rules:

1. Make sure that you understand thoroughly the passage **before** you paraphrase it. Note key words and phrases. Look up words you don't know.

2. Clarify and simplify as you paraphrase.

3. Retain the exact meaning of the original.

4. Maintain approximately the same length, order of ideas, tone, and message. Do not use the same words and phrases except for the few that cannot be changed because they have no adequate synonyms or because a specific word is essential to the meaning of the passage.

5. Develop and maintain your own writing style throughout the paper, even when restating others' ideas, attitudes, and beliefs.

6. Provide in-text citations for all paraphrased material.

Read the following paragraph from Stephen Jay Gould's essay "Of Kiwi Eggs and the Liberty Bell," which is on pages 111-112 of Gould's book <u>Bully for Brontosaurus</u>. Then examine both the proposed paraphrases and decide which one is acceptable and why.

> **Original:**
>
> But the greatest of kiwi oddities centers upon reproduction. Females are
>
> larger than males. They lay one to three eggs and may incubate them for a
>
> while, but they leave the nest soon thereafter, relegating to males the primary

task of incubation, a long seventy to eighty-four days. Males sit athwart the egg, body at a slight angle and bill stretched out along the ground. Females may return occasionally with food, but males must usually fend for them—selves, covering both eggs and nest entrance with debris and going forth to forage once or twice on most nights.

Pigpen's version:

> The oddest thing about kiwis is how they reproduce. Females are bigger than males. They lay a small number of eggs and then sit on them for a while, but then they leave and let the males take care of them, for as long as eighty-four days. Males sit on the egg angled slightly and stretching their bills out along the ground. Once in a while the females come back with food, but males must usually fend for themselves. They cover the eggs and the nest entrance with debris and go out to forage once or twice on most nights (Gould 111-112).

Linus's version:

> The most unusual aspect of kiwi behavior is their way of producing offspring. Females lay one to three eggs and may take care of them for a time, but they soon take off, leaving the smaller fathers to tend the eggs for as long as twelve weeks. The males perch on the egg, tilting forward and extending their beaks along the ground. Although the females sometimes bring some food to their mates, the males are mainly on their own. During the night they go out in search of sustenance after leaving some protective covering on the eggs and the approach to the nest (Gould 111-112).

When you compared, you probably noticed that Pigpen repeated many of the words of the original, using slightly different forms: oddest/oddities, reproduce/reproduction, angled slightly/slight angle. His paraphrase also repeats exactly sentences like "males must usually fend for themselves" and "[they] forage once or twice on most nights." After reviewing the rules, try paraphrasing the following paragraph from "The Horn of Triton," on pages 501-502 of the same book.

Practice:

Jane Goodall's quarter century with the chimpanzees of Gombe will rank forever as one of the great achievements in scientific dedication combined with stunning results. With such unprecedented, long-term knowledge of daily history, Goodall can specify (and quantify) the major determinants of her population's fate. Contrary to our intuitions and expectations, the demography of the Gombe chimps has not been set primarily by daily rhythms of birth, feeding, sex, and death, but by three "rare events" (Goodall's words), all involving mayhem or misfortune: a polio epidemic, a carnage of one sub-band by another, and the . . . tale of one peculiar individual.

Summarizing

A summary is a shortened version of a paraphrase. It retains the original writer's main idea and point of view but condenses the material. Like the paraphrase, it uses your own words. Here are the rules:

1. Read the passage, paying attention to key words and looking up words you don't know.
2. Restate the main facts and ideas, keeping the order.
3. Include essential information, but omit descriptive details, examples, illustrations, analogies, and anecdotes.
4. Try to shrink the passage to about one-third the length of the original.
5. Provide a parenthetical citation for the material you summarize.

Read the following paragraph by Melvin R. Gilmore, quoted on page 542 of <u>PrairyErth</u> by William Least Heat-Moon, and then compare the two summaries that follow. Do they convey the main idea of the original? Are any crucial points omitted? Has anything been added that was not in the original passage?

Original:

The common saying that the island of Manhattan was "purchased from the Indian inhabitants for the value of twenty-four dollars in traders' goods" is not true. It is not true for the reason that the Indians did not and could not think of the possibility of conveying property in land. What the Indians of Manhattan did conceive was the idea of admitting the Dutch sailors to live in the land with themselves as neighbors, to share its benefits. But they had no idea of selling the land for any price. No Indians of Manhattan or elsewhere entertained at any time any such idea. Indians always said in opposition to such proposals, "We cannot sell the land, for it belongs not to us in this generation only, but to all our people for all time. . . ." [The Indians] thought of the goods given by the Dutch as being merely presents given as a pledge and token of good will and neighborly relations. The idea of alienation of the land was never in their minds.

Lucy's version:

> The widely believed story that the Indians of Manhattan sold their island to the Dutch settlers for $24 is false. Selling land for any price was inconceivable to the Indians, who believed that the land belonged not only to them, but to their descendants as well. The Indians were willing to share their land with the Dutch, whose goods they considered gifts, signs of trust and neighborliness. But they never dreamed of selling their land (Heat-Moon 542).

Schroeder's version:

> It is not true that the island of Manhattan was "purchased from the Indian inhabitants for the value of 24 dollars" in beads and trinkets. The Indians never considered the possibility of trading or selling their land. Their idea was to let the Dutch settlers come and live with them as neighbors and share the wealth. But they had no intention of selling the land. They said, "We cannot sell the land, for it belongs not to us in this generation only, but to all our people for all time. . . ." The Indians considered the goods given by the Dutch just as presents but not as payment for the land (Heat-Moon 542).

After noting the differences between Lucy's and Schroeder's summaries and deciding which one is best and why, try summarizing the paragraph below. It is on pages 318-319 of the same book where the author quotes his anthropologist friend Joe Hickey, who is discussing the Native American nation, the Kansa (also called "the Kaw").

Practice:

> The standard argument has always been that the Kansa were among the most resistant and stupid of Indians and that they refused to give up traditional ways and accord themselves with Thomas Jefferson's idea for them as "Christian-farmers." But that argument is mostly a myth perpetrated by whites who made sure the Indians failed. Traders wanted them out hunting to supply the fur market, squatters and speculators wanted their land, missionaries wanted their souls, and bureaucrats wanted the power and money attached to sales of Indian land, so it became expedient to blame the Kaw themselves for lack of progress in learning how to farm. The myth also conveniently absolved whites from guilt and complicity in genocide. The Kaws' failure to leave old nomadic ways was almost foreordained by whites.[*]

Summary

Paraphrasing and Summarizing

- Paraphrase or summarize most of your borrowed material; use direct quotation sparingly.

- Clarify and simplify as you restate the essential ideas, facts, and conclusions of the original.

- Condense lengthy excerpts by omitting descriptive details, examples, quotations, and repetition.

---

[*] The cited material is from Stephen Jay Gould, <u>Bully for Brontosaurus: Reflections in Natural History</u> (New York: Norton, 1991), and William Least Heat-Moon, <u>PrairyErth</u> (Boston: Houghton, 1991).

Chapter 15
Using Direct Quotation

Use direct quotation where the author's exact wording is essential to convey his or her meaning, tone, or language use. Primary and secondary sources, mentioned below, are explained in Appendix B. Review the general rules first, and then look at the suggestions and examples for providing lead-ins and follow-ups for direct quotations. Because the process is complex, this chapter provides a number of examples from both student and professional writers.

General rules

    A. Use direct quotation of **secondary source** material:

        1. To show excellence of ideas and expression.

        2. To explain complex material.

        3. To provide a way of introducing your own observations.

    B. Use direct quotation of **primary source** material:

        1. To provide evidence for judgments about a poem, speech, novel, case study, historical analysis, and the like.

        2. To provide specific examples to support interpretation of symbolism, analysis of character, suggestion of theme, and the like.

    C. Copy the author's exact words and enclose them in quotation marks, following the rules for punctuation and capitalization:

        1 Place commas and periods **inside** quotation marks.

        2. Place colons, semi-colons, and dashes **outside** quotation marks.

        3. Place question marks or exclamation points **inside** quotation marks when they punctuate the quotation; place them **outside** when they punctuate the sentence.

        4. Use single quotation marks for a quotation within a quotation.

> Comparing Melville with Dana in regard to the albatross, Lawrence describes Melville as "a bit sententious— 'I remember the first albatross I ever saw. It was during a prolonged gale. . . .'"

Here the writer quotes Lawrence, who quotes Melville, to illustrate the point about sententiousness.

5. Alter initial capitals when a quotation forms a grammatical part of the sentence:

> Lawrence, however, claims that "only counterfeit emotions exist nowadays."

Otherwise, retain the capitalization in the quoted sentence:

> Elsewhere Lawrence declares, "That was the pin he tortured himself on, like a pinned-down butterfly."

D. For every direct quotation, provide:

   1. A **lead-in**, that is, introductory words or phrases.

   2. A **follow-up**, that is, an explanation of its meaning, relevance, or significance.

   3. A **parenthetical citation**, for example, ". . . to sleep forever" (Mudge 98).

E. Avoid monotony and maintain fluency by using a variety of methods to introduce direct quotations, e.g.:

   - A sharply contrasting attitude is that of Ralph Nader:

   - The distinguished literary critic Helen Vendler maintains . . .

   - According to Nobel Laureate Derek Walcott . . .

   - Noted economist Kenneth Galbraith presents a different point of view:

   - In support of this position, Senator Hillary Clinton (D-NY) argues . . .

F. Use ellipses, that is, three spaced dots, for omissions. If the author you are quoting uses ellipsis points, you may enclose your own ellipses in square brackets, [. . .] to distinguish yours from the author's.

Original Passage:

It was thus that He recovered from being a God. . . . He had made everything too beautiful. . . . The devil is simply God's moment of idleness at the end of that seventh day.

Direct quotation:

Explaining the serpent at the tree of knowledge, Friedrich Nietzsche writes: "It was thus that He recovered from being a God. . . . [. . .] The devil is simply God's moment of idleness at the end of that seventh day" (909).

G. Use [sic] to indicate the retention of errors in the original. For example, if you quote the sentence "The lost aviators poured [sic] over their maps," the bracketed word shows that you know the writer's use of "poured" is incorrect: it should be "pored." When you need to make a minor change in the wording of a direct quotation, for example, to change a pronoun or a verb tense, insert the needed word in brackets.

Original Passage:

And it must be understood that a prince, and especially a new prince, cannot observe all those things which are considered good in men, being often obliged, in order to maintain the state, to act against faith, against charity, against humanity, and against religion.

Direct quotation:

In explaining how the ruler must keep faith with his subjects, Machiavelli argues that "a prince, and especially a new prince, . . . [is] often obliged . . . to act against faith, against charity, against humanity, and against religion" (102-103).

H. For quotations that are longer than four lines, start a new line, indenting the entire quotation one inch from the left margin. Double space, omit quotation marks, and place the citation outside the closing punctuation.

Remember that most of your paper should be your own presentation of thoroughly assimilated material in which you use direct quotation **only sparingly**. Directly quoted material should constitute no more than 10% of the final paper.

Lead-Ins for Quotations in a Literary Analysis Essay

A.   **Choosing paraphrase or direct quotation** In an essay on a major theme in <u>The Catcher in the Rye</u>, Jessica writes the following topic sentence: Holden reveals his inability to accept responsibility and to behave in a mature way by refusing to take school seriously.

1. She could support this using **paraphrase:**

    a.

    > Holden explains that his present school, Pencey Prep, has just kicked him out for academic reasons (4).

    b.

    > He dropped out of two other schools, the Whooton School and Elkton Hills (13).

2. Or she could use **direct quotation:**

    a.

    > Holden explains that he isn't returning to Pencey Prep: "They kicked me out. I wasn't supposed to come back after Christmas vacation, on account of I was flunking four subjects and not applying myself and all. They gave me frequent warnings . . ." (4).

    b.

    > The reader learns about Holden's previous academic failures through his conversation with Mr. Spencer, who remarks, "If I'm not mistaken, I believe you had some difficulty at the Whooton School and at Elkton Hills" (13).

    c.

    > Holden explains why: "One of the biggest reasons I left Elkton Hills was because I was surrounded by phonies. . . . They were coming in the goddam window. For instance, they had this headmaster, Mr. Haas, that was the phoniest bastard I ever met in my life" (13-14).

B.   Rules for leading into direct quotations in literary analysis:

1. **Never** insert a direct quotation without a lead-in, that is, an introductory phrase indicating the speaker or explaining the context.

2. As in example 2a and 2c above, use a colon when the quotation is a complete sentence that is joined to another complete sentence.

3. As in example 2b, a comma is often appropriate after the lead-in when it indicates the speaker, as in: Stephen Pinker observes, "Philosophy today gets no respect"; or Jared Diamond laments, "Alas, some clever microbes don't just cave in to our immune defenses."

4. Often it is best to use only part of a direct quotation and to paraphrase the rest. For example:

   > Holden explains that he was "surrounded by phonies," and that he disliked the headmaster (13).

5. Use direct quotations **sparingly** and only when necessary to convey your meaning. Use longer quotations **only** when they are essential in a discussion of diction, imagery, syntax, or other elements that you must exemplify in order to discuss them clearly. For example, if Jessica is discussing Holden's moment of illumination at the carousel, when he realizes that adults must let children grow up, she might need to quote the entire passage if that is a major point in her essay. She might write:

   > Almost at the end of the story, Holden has a moment of illumination when he realizes that adults must let children grow up. He observes:
   >
   > > All the kids kept trying to grab the gold ring, and so was old Phoebe, and I was sort of afraid she'd fall off the goddam horse, but I didn't say anything or do anything. The thing with kids is, if they want to grab for the gold ring, you have to let them do it, and not say anything. If they fall off, they fall off, but it's bad if you say anything to them. (211)

Notice that Jessica has omitted quotation marks, indented the entire passage, used double spacing, and placed the citation outside the closing punctuation. She would start a new paragraph for her discussion of the quotation.

Lead-Ins from a Professional Writer

The following examples are from an article in the <u>Atlantic Monthly</u>, "Was the Great War Necessary?" by Benjamin Schwartz, in which the author reviews <u>The Pity of War</u> by Niall Ferguson. The discussion is about World War I.

1. Lead-ins often provide the **credentials** of the person being quoted, thus establishing his or her authority in the field.

> Moreover, as dreadful as was Britain's experience, "the disturbing paradox" of the Great War was, according to the historian J. M. Winter, that it was at once "an event of unparalleled carnage and suffering and the occasion of a significant improvement in the life expectancy of the civilian population . . ." (Schwartz 119).
>
> In short, the goal was, in the words of the historian Imanuel Geiss, whom Ferguson quotes approvingly, "German leadership over a united Europe in order to brave the coming giant economic and political power blocs" (122).

2. The skillful placement of attributions can help careful writers avoid the repetitiousness of continual "He saids" and "She writes." Schwartz also illustrates how one can integrate direct quotations into one's text smoothly and economically.

Reviewing a war memoir in 1920, one critic plaintively sought some purpose behind the conflict: "Nowhere will you find a period or a sentence of which you could say, 'There! That is what we fought for!' The Cause finds no expression" (120).

Wilson stated his position clearly at the outset of his book: "Britain's involvement in the Great War was not some deplorable accident" (120).

As Ferguson acknowledges, Germany "forced the continental war of 1914 upon an unwilling France (and a not so unwilling Russia)" (122).

So they had come to believe, as the diplomat Sir Eyre Crowe put it, that "the building of the German fleet is but one of the symptoms of the disease. It is the political ambitions of the German Government and nation which are the source of the mischief" (123).

But those British generals, diplomats, and politicians . . . were hardly brimming with optimism—as Sir Edward Grey's oft-quoted lament, delivered on the eve of the war, attests: "The lamps are going out all over Europe; we shall not see them lit again in our lifetime" (128).

Providing Follow-Ups of Direct Quotations

The main idea:

A direct quotation does not speak for itself. The writer usually must follow it up with explanation, discussion, or commentary instead of abandoning the quotation and letting it twist in the wind. Such commentary may focus on the significance of the quoted material, its implications, its relevance to the writer's argument, or its application to the topic under discussion. Follow-up sentences never paraphrase the quotation nor do they take the form, "This quotation means . . ." or "The writer is saying . . ." Follow-up remarks add something worth saying to the discussion, often developing or amplifying the ideas the quotation expresses.

Example 1   Henry Kissinger writes:

> Over 540,000 American troops were fighting in Viet Nam, and our country was tearing itself apart over what Professor Walter A. McDougall of the University of Pennsylvania has brilliantly described as America's first "Great Society war." By this he meant that Viet Nam was the first American war fought for no military objective. Rather, the strategic goal was not to lose in order to give South Viet Nam time to create democratic institutions and social programs that would win the war for the hearts and minds of the population.

The author realizes that the reader may not understand the meaning of McDougal's phrase "Great Society war," so Kissinger provides an explanation. Please note: "By this he meant" is poor style, showing that even professional writers sometimes err. The follow-up, however, is excellent because it clarifies an unfamiliar concept.

Example 2   Discussing H. D. Thoreau's unnerving visit to Mt. Katahdin in 1846, Bill Bryson writes:

> This wasn't the tame world of overgrown orchards and sun-dappled parks that passed for wilderness in suburban Concord, Massachusetts, but a forbidding, oppressive, primeval country that was "grim and wild . . . savage and dreary," fit only for "men nearer of kin to the rocks and wild animals than we." The experience left him, in the words of one biographer, "near hysterical." But even men far tougher and more attuned to the wilderness than Thoreau were sobered by its strange and palpable menace.

Bryson does not merely quote the words in Thoreau's description of the Maine wilderness. He goes beyond the quotation, providing more detail, and he adds that Thoreau's reaction, far from being unusual, was a common one at the time.

Example 3   Barbara Tuchman writes:

> Recognizing the prospect of siege, Cornwallis wrote Clinton as Commander-in-Chief on September 16-17, "If you cannot relieve me very soon, you must be prepared to hear the worst." The "worst" was left ambiguous. If the "worst" meant defeat or surrender, it must be inferred that Cornwallis, without a ready source of provisions, had no intention of fighting his way out by land.

Because the reader may not understand what "worst" means in this context, Tuchman explains what it means and what its implications were for the participants in this event. She provides a necessary amplification of the information in the quotation.

Example 4   Adam Hochschild writes:

> "Those who are conquered," wrote the philosopher Ibn Khaldun in the fourteenth century, "always want to imitate the conqueror in his main characteristics—in his clothing, his crafts, and in all his distinctive traits and customs." Mobutu's luxurious Villa del Mare, a pink-and-white marble colonnaded chateau at Roquebrune-Cap-Martin on the French Riviera, complete with indoor and outdoor swimming pools, gold-fitted bathrooms, and heliport, lay a mere dozen miles down the coast from the estates Leopold once owned at Cap Ferrat.

Hochschild's follow-up provides specific details and examples that bring out the significance of the quotation. He shows the relevance of the fourteenth century philosopher's statement by citing contemporary evidence and connecting it to his argument about the role of forced labor in colonial expansion.

Example 5   In an article about Richard Henry Dana, Castle Freeman, Jr. writes:

> Reflecting on the great adventure of his youth and his life-long love of seafaring and distant lands, [Dana] wrote that he had been "lucky in travel, though in nothing else." He probably understood that he would be remembered, not for what he regarded as his real work, but for <u>Two Years before the Mast</u>, which he was apt to dismiss as "a boy's book" and regarded as the product of "a parenthesis in my life."

The quotation from Dana would have been confusing without Freeman's follow-up. He explains that the "lucky in travel" is a reference to the youthful adventures that led to Dana's famous book, while "in nothing else" alludes to his failure to achieve fame and success in his life work, the law and public service. Freeman closes his short biographical piece with the above paragraph. It works because he has chosen his quotation from Dana wisely, and he has followed it up with the needed explanation.

Summary

Direct Quotation

- Choose direct quotations wisely, based on relevance, grace of expression, and aptness.

- Paraphrase or summarize most of your borrowed material rather than using direct quotation.

- Always introduce a direct quotation by identifying the speaker, mentioning a cited authority's credentials, or providing the context. **Never** insert a direct quotation without an introductory phrase. **Never, ever.**

- Make sure you have quoted correctly, including spelling and punctuation. Use ellipses to show omissions; avoid quoting long passages.

- Follow up a direct quotation with an explanation, commentary, or clarification, as appropriate. Do not assume that the quotation can stand by itself. It can't.

Chapter 16A
Parenthetical Documentation MLA

This chapter addresses parenthetical documentation, one of the most popular methods of showing, within the text of your paper, the exact sources of your information and of giving credit to the author. It goes hand in hand with providing a complete list of the sources you used, the works cited page, formerly called the bibliography, and is an essential step in your on-going campaign to avoid plagiarism. Although there are other methods of citing sources, this is one of the best.

You **must** provide parenthetical documentation whenever you:

- Use a direct quotation.

- Paraphrase, that is, express in your own words, ideas or opinions that are not your own original thoughts.

- Summarize in your own words information or ideas.

> **Note:**
> You must also give the source of a map, table, chart, graph, illustration, or diagram, but this information is placed under the figure rather than in the text.

You do **not** need documentation for an idea or information that is:

- Your own opinion, arrived at independently. For example:

    Snowboarding attracts more risk-takers than does downhill skiing.

- Common knowledge or an undisputed fact. For example:

    Columbus sailed west in 1492 in the hope of discovering a new route to Asia.

To provide parenthetical documentation, give the source, usually just the author's last name and the page number, within parentheses, after the borrowed material in your paper.

> During the Middle Ages, people thought of the labyrinth in art as something enjoyable, exemplifying both God's creation and human artistry (Doob 144).

The parenthetical citation— (Doob 144)—shows that the information about this view of labyrinths comes from page 144 of a book by Doob. The works cited page at the end of your paper will provide complete publication information about this book.

Works cited entry

> Doob, Penelope Reed. The Idea of the Labyrinth from Classical Antiquity through the Middle Ages. Ithaca: Cornell UP, 1990.

Guidelines for Parenthetical Documentation

1. General

    a. The information in **parenthetical citations** must match the corresponding information on the **works cited** page.

    b. The parenthetical citation usually appears **at the end of the sentence**, as close as possible to the material it documents, so that it does not interrupt the flow of the writing.

    c. To cite an entire work, you need only include the author's name in the text.

> Justus Buchler expounds this view in The Main of Light.

No parenthetical citation follows, but complete information appears on the works cited page.

Works Cited entry

> Buchler, Justus. The Main of Light: On the Concept of Poetry. New York: Oxford UP, 1974.

    d. If the author's name appears in a sentence in your paper, then you should **not** repeat it in the citation:

> Orwell made this point earlier in "Shooting an Elephant" (65-66).

    e. If you cite the same author twice in succession, then omit the author's name in the second citation, using the page number only.

> He accepts a sad truth: "History is made by warfare, greed, lust for power, hatred, and xenophobia. . ." (Gould 280). But he wishes to argue that aggressiveness and selfishness by no means define the human being. On the contrary, one must factor in the "ten thousand ordinary acts of kindness" that characterize human experience (282).

If you cite a different author in between, however, you must include Gould's name again in the second citation:

> He accepts a sad truth: "History is made by warfare, greed, lust for power, hatred, and xenophobia. . ." (Gould 280). But he wishes to argue that aggressiveness and selfishness by no means define the human being. On the contrary, concern for others appeared early in human history, as exemplified by the Neanderthals' practice of caring for their sick (Diamond 38). One must factor in the "ten thousand ordinary acts of kindness" that characterize human experience (Gould 282), rather than assuming that our tendency toward violence is a biological necessity.

f. Parenthetical citations should be as **brief** and as **few** as clarity and accuracy permit. Give only the essential information, and do not add parenthetical references unnecessarily.

g. The parenthetical citation normally **precedes the punctuation mark** that concludes the sentence, clause, or phrase containing the borrowed material.

> In his essay on cannibals, Montaigne mentions the disappearance of the great island of Atlantis (138-140).

h. If a direct quotation occurs **at the end of the sentence**, insert the parenthetical citation between the closing quotation mark and the concluding punctuation mark.

> He concludes his review of Anne Tyler's latest book with the declaration, "This writer is not merely good, she is <u>wickedly</u> good" (Updike 278).

i. In an extended quotation of **more than four typed lines**, which is indented one inch or ten spaces and is typed double-spaced, the citation follows the last line of the quotation and is placed outside the ending punctuation.

> In <u>A Distant Mirror</u>, Barbara Tuchman alludes to the traditional personification of Death:
>
> > A skeleton with hourglass and scythe, in a white shroud or bare-boned, grinning at the irony of man's fate reflected in his image: that all men, from beggar to emperor, from harlot to queen, from ragged clerk to Pope, must come to this. No matter what their poverty or power in life, all is vanity, equalized in death. (124)

2. Additional Rules and Examples

a. In a paper based on a **single primary source**, for example, a novel, play, or poem, most teachers are satisfied if you give just the page number or line number in parentheses following the referenced material. In a paper on <u>The Catcher in the Rye</u>, your citation would look like this:

> After watching Phoebe riding on the carousel, Holden realizes that adults must let children take chances. He concludes, "If they fall off, they fall off, but it's bad if you say anything to them" (211).

b. If your works cited list contains **only one work by the author**, give only the author's last name:

>   (Morgan 210).

c. If your list contains **two authors with the same last name**, include the first initial of the author cited:

>   (P. Morgan 42-44) for Percy and (R. Morgan 176) for Regina.

If you have two P. Morgans—Peter and Paula—then you must include first names.

>   (Peter Morgan 65). (Paula Morgan 119).

d. If one work has **two or three authors**, include the last name of each:

>   (Hart, Schafner, and Marx 35).

e. If one work has **three or more authors**, use the last name of the first author, followed by et al., with no intervening punctuation:

> (Williams et al. 109-112).

f. If the work has a **corporate author**, e.g., Government Printing Office or American Library Association, use that name, shortened if possible:

> (GPO 89). (ALA 356-360).

g. If the work is listed by **its title only**, use the title, shortened if possible:

> (Guidelines)

> ("Pelican")

h. If your list contains **more than one work by an author**, give the title, shortened if possible, with a comma only between the author's name and the work:

> (Chin, History 435)

> (Chin, Dragons 67)

i. If citing a **multivolume work**, give volume as well as page number(s), placing a colon between volume and page number:

> (Hume 4: 400-407).

The citation for an entire volume looks like this:

> (Schlesinger, vol. 4).

j. The citation for a classic literary work, for example, To the Lighthouse by Virginia Woolf, may also include chapter numbers. Give the page number first, followed by a semicolon, and then the chapter, using appropriate abbreviations:

> (Woolf 195; chap. 2).

> (273; chap. 3).

k. In citations for classic verse plays and poems, omit page numbers and cite by division (act, scene, canto, book, part) and line. Use periods to separate these numbers. To cite act 5, scene 1, line 101 in Hamlet, write:

> (Hamlet 5.1.101).

To cite lines in canto 17 of Dante's Inferno, write:

> (Inferno 17.1-26).

l. Citations for the Bible and other religious works omit page numbers but include book, chapter, and line numbers.

> (Exod. 14:19-25).

A citation for sura 54 of the Koran would read:

> (Koran 54.33-55).

m. When citing electronic sources, give the author's name and page number or paragraph number, if the latter is used.

(Gordon par. 25)

If the source lacks numbering, omit numbers from your parenthetical references. Do not include the page numbers of a printout from the Web since these may vary.

(Martindale)

n. You may omit page numbers in citations of entire works, encyclopedia articles, non-print sources, or one-page works.

o. You may combine **two sources in one citation** where appropriate; separate them with a semi-colon:

(Tinker 48; Evers 90).

(Evers 129; Chance 74).

Summary

Parenthetical Citations—MLA

- Parenthetical citations are required for all borrowed material, whether paraphrased, summarized, or quoted directly. Maps, charts, diagrams, and the like require source information under the figure.

- Place the parentheses at the end of the material cited; include the author's surname and the page number(s).

- Consult the detailed guidelines for rules about multiple authors and other specific cases, and also for punctuation rules.

- Keep parenthetical citations as brief and as few as accuracy permits.

- Make sure that your in-text citations match **exactly** the corresponding information on your works cited page.

Chapter 16B
Parenthetical Documentation APA

This chapter explains how to provide reference citations throughout your text. This is the accepted method of showing the exact sources of your information and of giving credit to the authors. It enables the reader to locate information in the complete list of the sources used, the alphabetical reference list at the end of your article. Both steps are essential in your on-going campaign to avoid plagiarism.

You **must** provide parenthetical documentation whenever you:

- Use a direct quotation.
- Paraphrase, that is, express in your own words, ideas, or opinions that are not your own original thoughts.
- Summarize in your own words information or ideas.

> **Note:**
> You must also give the source of a map, table, chart, graph, illustration, or diagram, but this information is placed in the caption or under the figure.

You do **not** need documentation for an idea or information that is:

- Your own opinion, arrived at independently. For example:

    Snowboarding attracts more risk-takers than does downhill skiing.

- Common knowledge or an undisputed fact. For example:

    Sigmund Freud is the founder of the psychoanalytic movement.

To provide parenthetical documentation, use the author–date method of citation, that is, give the surname of the author and the year of publication, inserted in the text at the appropriate point.

> Many young auto thieves described their motivation to steal as the desire for thrills and excitement, including the fun of police chases, rather than the urge to make money (Copes, 2003).

The citation—(Copes, 2003)—shows that the information about this type of street crime comes from an article by Copes that appeared in 2003. The references page at the end of your paper will provide complete publication information.

References entry

> Copes, H. (2003). Streetlife and the rewards of auto theft. Deviant Behavior, 24, 309-332.

Guidelines for Reference Citations in the Text

1. **General**

   a. The information in reference citations in the text must match the corresponding information in the **reference list**.

   b. The reference citation is inserted in **midsentence**, or **at the end of the sentence**, as close as possible to the material it documents.

   c. If the author's name appears in a sentence in your paper, do **not** repeat it in the citation.

   > Bychowski (1968) observed that survivors often experienced withdrawal, indifference, listlessness, or constant agitation.

   d. Reference citations should be as **brief** and as **few** as clarity and accuracy permit. Give only the required information, and do not add parenthetical references unnecessarily.

   e. The reference citation at the end of a sentence **precedes the punctuation mark** that concludes the sentence, clause, or phrase containing the borrowed material.

   > Some survivors suffered from a distorted sense of time, perhaps the result of having lost five years of their lives to the camps (Berger, 1988).

f. If a direct quotation occurs **at the end of the sentence**, insert the reference citation between the closing quotation mark and the concluding punctuation mark.

> A research psychologist described this condition as one of "total apathy and resignation . . . of wordless sadness" (Niederland, 1988, p. 8).

g. An extended quotation of **more than 40 words** is known as a **block quotation**. It is indented five spaces and is typed double-spaced, without quotation marks. The citation follows the last word of the quotation and is placed outside the ending punctuation.

> Lazarus and Folkman (1984) illustrate this point with an example from Lucas's (1969) study of coal miners who failed to recognize a potential threat:
>
> > Reports of the miners interviewed after the rescue from a mine explosion and subsequent entrapment indicated that they failed to recognize the danger of running out of water and the need to conserve it while they searched for an exit. Although cut off, the miners apparently did not foresee the possibility of being trapped for a long period. After two days of searching for an exit, their water supply was exhausted and they were forced to drink their urine in order to survive.
> > (p. 186)

2. Additional Rules and Examples

a. If your reference list contains **only one work by one author**, give only the date, or the author's last name and the date.

> Morgenstern (1998) compared the effects of biofeedback and drug therapy.

> A recent study of the effects of biofeedback and drug therapy (Morgenstern, 1998) produced equally puzzling results.

> Gould (1993) observed that this principle "works just as well for the mental complexities of emotions and intelligence as for designs of entire bodies" (p. 255).

b. If your list contains **two primary authors with the same surname**, include the first author's initials in all text citations, even if the year of publication differs.

> R. P. Stern (1985) and H. D. Stern (1990) also studied this effect.

c. If one work has **two authors**, always cite both names every time a reference occurs in the text.

> (Eig & Bacon, 1998)

d. If one work has **three, four, or five authors**, cite all authors the first time a reference occurs; in subsequent citations, include only the surname of the first author followed by "et al." (not italicized and with a period after "al") and the year if it is the first reference within a paragraph.

> Williams, Wasserstein, Brown, and Chu (1992) found [first citation]
>
> Williams et al. (1992) found [subsequent first citation per paragraph]
>
> Williams et al. found [omit date from subsequent citations after first in paragraph]

e. When a work has **six or more authors**, cite only the surname of the first author followed by "et al." (not italicized and with a period after "al") and the year for the first and subsequent citations.

> Sanchez et al. (1997) also found

If two references with six or more authors shorten to the same form, cite the surnames of the first authors and as many subsequent authors as necessary to distinguish the two references.

f. If the work has a **group as author**, e.g., corporations, associations, government agencies, and study groups, the names are usually spelled out each time they appear in a text citation. The names of some group authors are spelled out the first time and abbreviated thereafter.

> (National Institute of Mental Health [NIMH], 1997) [first text citation]
>
> (NIMH, 1997) [subsequent text citations]

g. If the work has **no author**, cite in text the first few words of the reference list entry (usually the title) and the year. Use double quotation marks around the title of an article or chapter, and italicize the title of a periodical, book, brochure, or report.

> on managed care ("Study Finds," 1985)
>
> the book <u>Community Service Opportunities</u> (1994)

If the work's author is designated as "Anonymous," cite in text the word <u>Anonymous,</u> followed by a comma and the date:

> (Anonymous, 1991)

h. Arrange **two or more works within the same parentheses** in the same order in which they appear in the reference list. Arrange two or more works by the same authors by year of publication. Place in-press citations last. Give the authors' surnames once; for each subsequent work, give only the date.

> Past research (Evans & Winston, 1992, 1995)
>
> Past research (Garcia, 1995; 2004, in press)

i. If your list contains **more than one work by the same author** (or by the same two or more authors in the same order) with the same publication date, identify the works by the suffixes a, b, c, and so forth after the year; repeat the year.

> Several studies (Fitzmartin & Jacobsen, 1998a, 1998b, 1998c; Rishi, 2001, in press-a, in press-b) support this view.

j. List **two or more works by different authors** who are cited within the same parentheses in alphabetical order by the first author's surname. Separate the citations by semi-colons.

> Several studies (Boynton, 1979; Hassam, 1982; Jossine & Watson, 1986)
>
> Exception: (Rankin, 1990; see also Abel, 1994; Sturm, 1997)

k. To cite specific parts of a source, give the page, chapter, figure, table, or equation at the appropriate place in the text. For quotations, always provide page numbers. Page and chapter are abbreviated in in-text citations.

> (Yeoman & Elson, 2000, p. 178)
>
> (Dangerfield, 1989, chap. 5)

l. To cite **specific parts of an electronic source** where no page numbers are provided, use the paragraph number, if available, preceded by the ¶ symbol or the abbreviation para. If neither paragraph nor page numbers are visible, cite the heading and the number of the paragraph following it.

> As Mingus (2001, ¶4) points out,
>
> (Bloch, 2001, Conclusion section, para. 3)

m. **Personal communications** may be letters, memos, some electronic communications (e.g., e-mail, messages from nonarchived discussion groups or electronic bulletin boards), personal interviews, telephone conversations, and the like. Do not include them in the reference list; cite them in the text only. Give the initials as well as the surname of the communicator, and provide as exact a date as possible.

> M. K. Milligan (personal communication, August 14, 2003)
>
> W. P. Mui (personal communication, February 7, 2004)

n. In **citations in parenthetical material**, use commas, not brackets, to set off the date.

> (see Table 2 of Weed, Saunders, & Wright, 1998, for complete data)

Summary

Parenthetical Citations—APA

- Parenthetical citations are required for all borrowed material, whether paraphrased, summarized, or quoted directly; maps, charts, diagrams and the like require source information under the figure.

- Place the parentheses close to the material cited; include the author's surname and the year of publication.

- Consult the detailed guidelines for rules about multiple authors and other specific cases, and also for punctuation rules.

- Keep parenthetical citations as brief and as few as accuracy permits.

- Make sure that your in-text citations match **exactly** the corresponding information on your reference list.

Chapter 17
Using Titles Correctly

In most research papers, the writer refers to many different works, both in the text and in the documentation. It is important that you refer to books, newspapers, essays, short stories, reviews, journal articles, and the like correctly. This chapter gives the rules you need for capitalizing and punctuating, following MLA style.

The MLA Handbook favors underlining rather than italics in student research papers, although in a published paper, underlined words would usually be printed in italics. On the other hand, the APA Publication Manual favors italicizing titles in manuscripts intended for publication, but it allows underlining if the writer lacks the italics function. You should ask your teacher which format he or she prefers, and then be consistent. In this manual we use underlining because it is more conspicuous; italicized words are easy to overlook. Unlike italics, underlining is available when you must use handwriting, as on source and note cards.

Rule 1. In a title, **capitalize the first and last words, and all principal words in between,** including those that follow hyphens. In other words, capitalize all words in the middle of the title except articles (a, an, the); prepositions (against, between, in, of, to); coordinating conjunctions (and, but, for, nor, or, so, yet); and <u>to</u> in infinitives.

> America's Rail-Trails
>
> Blood Knot and Other Plays
>
> The House on Mango Street
>
> How to Raise Pumpkins

Rule 2. Where a **subtitle** follows a book's title, include the subtitle, joining it to the main title with a colon and a space.

> Speech: Its Function and Development
>
> Storytelling and Mythmaking: Images from Film and Literature
>
> Breaking Ice: An Anthology of Contemporary African-American Fiction

Rule 3. **Underline or use italics** for the titles of books, plays, long poems, pamphlets, periodicals (newspapers, magazines, journals), films, radio and television programs, compact discs, audiocassettes, record albums, ballets, operas and other long musical compositions, paintings, works of sculpture, ships, aircraft, and spacecraft.

The Catcher in the Rye (book)

A Raisin in the Sun (play)

Mahabharata (long poem)

Wall Street Journal (newspaper)

Rolling Stone (magazine)

Return of the King (film)

West Wing (television program)

An Evening Wasted with Tom Lehrer (compact disc)

Treasury of Walt Whitman: Leaves of Grass, 1 (audiocassette)

American Graffiti—41 Original Hits from the Sound Track (record album)

Les Sylphides (ballet)

Nixon in China (opera)

Symphonie fastastique (symphony not identified solely by numbers)

Garden of Earthly Delights (painting)

Seated Female Figure (Quimbaya) (sculpture)

USS Colorado (ship)

Friendship (aircraft)

Opportunity (spacecraft)

Rule 4. Use **quotation marks** for the titles of works published within larger works, for example, the titles of articles, essays, short stories, short poems, chapters of books, and individual episodes of television and radio programs.

"Legal Confusion over Gay Marriage" (newspaper article)

"Michael Moore's Art and Anger" (magazine article)

"Iran" (encyclopedia article)

"The Gangster As Tragic Hero" (essay)

"A Woman's Place" (short story)

"Duet on Mars" (poem)

"America Betrays Herself in Vietnam" (chapter in a book)

"Shadow" (episode of the television program Law and Order)

"Mood Indigo" (song)

"Black Books: The First African American Writers" (lecture)

Rule 5. **Underline** a title normally indicated by underlining (or use italics) when it appears within a title enclosed in quotation marks.

"<u>The Great Gatsby</u>: Thirty-Six Years After" (article about the novel)

Rule 6. **Use quotation marks** around a title normally indicated by quotation marks when it appears within an underlined (or italicized) title.

"<u>The Lottery" and Other Stories</u> (book of short stories)

Rule 7. **Enclose in single quotation marks** a title normally indicated by quotation marks when it appears within another title requiring quotation marks.

"Two objections to Quine's 'Two Dogmas.'" (article about an essay)

"A Comparison of 'Hawk Roosting' and 'Evening Hawk'" (essay about two poems)

Rule 8. Do not underline (or italicize) or enclose in quotation marks a normally underlined title when it appears within an underlined title. Make sure, however, that your text makes clear where the title ends and your writing begins.

<u>Approaches to Teaching Achebe's</u> Things Fall Apart (book about a book)

Rule 9. Do not underline (or italicize) or enclose within quotation marks the following: names of sacred writings; of laws, acts, and similar political documents; of instrumental musical compositions identified by form, number, and key; of series, societies, buildings, and monuments; and of conferences, seminars, workshops, and courses.

Bible, Genesis, Talmud, Koran, Upanishads (sacred writing)

Declaration of Independence, Magna Carta, Bill of Rights (political document)

Beethoven's Symphony no. 7 in A, op. 92; Brahms's Piano Concerto no. 2 in B flat, op. 83 (instrumental musical composition)

Bollingen Series, Masterpiece Theater (series)

American Philosophical Association, Jane Austen Society (society)

Empire State Building, Arc de Triomphe (building)

Re-Imagining the Welfare State; Battling for Ownership of the Arts (conference)

Exception:
Underline titles of individual published editions of sacred writings and include them with other published works in the works cited list, as in the following examples:

<u>The Jewish Study Bible: Tanakh Translation, Torah, Nevi'Im, Kethuvim</u>

<u>What the Koran Really Says: Language, Text, and Commentary</u>

Rule 10.   Words that indicate the divisions of a work are neither underlined, enclosed in quotation marks, nor capitalized when they are used in the text, as in statements such as "In their preface to <u>Stress, Appraisal, and Coping</u>, the authors write . . ." or "Marcel presents this idea in act 2 of <u>Ariadne</u>." Also in this list: introduction, list of works cited, bibliography, appendix, index, chapter 7, scene 2, stanza 14, canto 29.*

---

* Note that Chapters 9B and 20B give the APA rules for capitalizing titles in the reference list. The rules for titles in the text are different, and they are quite similar to the MLA rules. Here they are: Capitalize major words in titles of books and articles, that is, all words except conjunctions, articles, and short prepositions; but capitalize all words that are four letters or longer. If the first word in a hyphenated compound is capitalized, then capitalize the second. Capitalize the first word after a dash or a colon. You must keep in mind that the rules for capitalizing titles in the reference list are different.

Chapter 18
The Introduction and Conclusion

Although you've finished the body of your paper, you're not quite ready to celebrate. Your paper needs a snappy start and a satisfying close. This chapter explains how to write your introductory and concluding paragraphs.

The introduction

There are many ways to begin. Regardless of which approach you choose, the introductory paragraphs of a research paper usually include the following three elements:

1. Focusing sentences

   - Direct the reader's attention to the topic of the paper.

   - Are sometimes called the **grabber**, because their purpose is to "grab" the reader's attention.

   - Should not be painfully obvious or trite generalizations. Starting with "Albert Einstein was a great scientist" or "Life has its ups and downs" will induce instant sleep in your reader. Dictionary definitions are also stunningly boring.

   - Should consist of several thought-provoking, original sentences that will draw the reader into the discussion.

2. Thesis statement

   - Is the carefully worded statement of the main idea of the paper; never begins, "In this paper I will . . ."

   - Almost always includes a judgment or evaluation; is never merely a statement of fact.

   - May come right after the focusing sentences, or may come near the end of the thesis paragraph.

3. Method of development (MOD)

- Is a **brief** indication of the main topics that the author will use to support the thesis statement. It is like a blueprint.

- Is the writer's own work; it contains nothing borrowed.

- Should be followed by several additional sentences to bring the introductory paragraph(s) to a satisfactory close.

Experienced writers include these three elements in their opening paragraphs, but they often do more: they establish a tone, and they make a special effort to engage the reader's attention from the outset. A few of the techniques they sometimes use are listed below.

4. Additional techniques to add zip to your introduction:

- An entertaining anecdote, story, conversation, or example

- A strong, controversial opinion that opposes common assumptions or critical views

- An unusual or startling fact; surprising statistics or data

- A witty or humorous observation, if appropriate for the subject under discussion

- A dramatic, fascinating quotation, adage, or proverb

Examples of excellent introductory paragraphs

1. This paragraph introduces a literary study in which Brian traces the major influences on the author Ernest Hemingway.

> Many different influences affect a writer's development. Friends, family, locale, literary heroes, teachers—all may leave an imprint. In the case of Ernest Hemingway, although his experience as a reporter helped shape his style, other authors and their work exerted the major influence on Hemingway's work as a whole. His early writing owes much to several Americans, most notably, Sherwood Anderson. Mark Twain, whom Hemingway admired greatly, was also influential. And Gertrude Stein's ruthless criticism of his manuscripts helped him to write more succinctly. In the end, the Nobel laureate owed many debts to both his predecessors and his contemporaries.

2. This is how Meg began her biographical paper on Marie Curie. Meg's paper shows how Curie overcame many formidable obstacles to become a world famous scientist.

Throughout history, it has been difficult for women to achieve world renown. This is especially true, until recently, in fields such as mathematics and science. But Marie Curie, who lived from 1867 to 1934, won acclaim for her discoveries in chemistry and physics. She struggled against poverty and discrimination to obtain an excellent education, and then through years of hard work, she made important contributions to her field. Twice honored with the Nobel Prize, she is one of the most important women in the history of science.

3. The next paragraph is from a position paper on censorship. Ava began her paper as follows:

In writing children's literature, authors beg a difficult favor of parents. Beyond asking the opportunity to entertain or educate children, these writers seek access to the ultimate artistic medium: a forming mind. Ideas and perspectives that books introduce to young readers can have immeasurable impact, a fact that requires competent parents and schools to scrutinize children's books before presenting them to impressionable readers. School officials, at the same time, have a responsibility to recognize the value in certain works, despite the controversy they inspire. Revolting Rhymes by Roald Dahl is such a book. Although the macabre poems of Dahl's collection may not be appropriate for children in elementary school, educators should permit older students to read the book.

4. This introductory paragraph is from Rick's informative speech on the popularity of roller coasters. It uses concrete detail and specific information to take the audience to the main question that the speech addresses: Why are roller coasters so immensely popular? Notice that Rick has combined his thesis statement and MOD, an acceptable practice as long as the resulting sentence does not become too long and confusing.

From Riverfront Park in Spokane, Washington, to Busch Gardens in Tampa, Florida, the roller coaster dominates the scene. Whether it is the shuttle loop of the Viper at Six Flags over Georgia, or the mildly tot-terrorizing Kiddie Coaster at Playland in Rye, New York, the roller coaster has been the star attraction at amusement parks since 1886. The success of this ride is no accident. It took years of experimentation and constant improvement to build roller coasters that would provide maximum thrills without endangering lives. Today the coaster's overwhelming popularity in amusement parks around the world is the result of ingenious design, engineering skill, and the application of psychology.

The Conclusion

The concluding paragraphs of a paper bring it to a satisfactory close. They usually include:

1. Several sentences that refocus attention and signal the end.

2. **A reworded thesis statement** A reminder—<u>not a word-for-word repetition</u>—of the main idea of the paper, that is, a judgment, decision, argument, resolution, or the like..

3. **A recapitulation**—a concise summary of the major topics covered.

4. Concluding sentences that go beyond the thesis, often by doing one of the following:

   - providing a new insight or perspective
   - suggesting logical implications or practical consequences of the position stated
   - challenging the reader to take action or change behavior through specific proposals
   - showing how this view or discovery fits into the larger picture
   - making a prediction about future developments in this particular field
   - raising additional questions about the topic or suggesting the direction that future investigation might take

- mentioning a noteworthy incident, surprising statistic, apt quotation, or striking contrast that reinforces the main point of the essay

- offering a personal reflection

A good conclusion:

- Leaves the reader with a strong impression, a definite attitude

- Does not merely repeat.

- Does not begin "In conclusion" or "Finally." All but the dimmest reader can see that the end is in sight.

- Is the author's own work and does not contain any borrowed material except possibly a brief, highly appropriate quotation.

- Reflects the introduction by alluding to the same idea, saying, anecdote, or incident mentioned earlier.

Examples of excellent conclusions

1. Brian concluded his paper on Hemingway like this:

> Ernest Hemingway's mature style reflects his experience as a journalist as well as his admiration for such writers as Sherwood Anderson, Stephen Crane, and Mark Twain. It also shows the influence of Gertrude Stein, who for a brief time was Hemingway's mentor and critic. Yet despite these influences, Hemingway developed and perfected his own style, and in the end, distanced himself from other American writers. In terms of both style and content, he was truly his own person. His many excellent short stories and his finest novels continue the tradition of American literature and also make an original contribution to it.

2. Meg's concluding paragraph is the following:

> Throughout her education and career in physics and chemistry, Marie Curie showed the determination and willingness to work hard that made her a world class scientist. Her work in radioactivity and her discovery of several elements won her fame and culminated in the highest honors that a scientist can win. In the years following Curie's first Nobel Prize in 1903, only nine other women have become Nobel laureates in science, further evidence of the extraordinary nature of her achievement. Decades after her death in 1934, Curie still provides inspiration to those who pursue scientific truth, and especially to women.

3. Ava ended her paper with this paragraph:

> There is little doubt that Revolting Rhymes is unsuitable for elementary school children. In producing such a grotesque collection of poems and pictures, Roald Dahl and Quentin Blake compromised a portion of their potential audience. However, the book's offending feature, Dahl's biting, sardonic humor, is precisely what endears Revolting Rhymes to older children. In concentrating their efforts on a specific age group, both writer and illustrator establish a unique connection with their young readers and intensify the effect of their art. Revolting Rhymes, unrepentant vulgarity and all, thrills its target audience in a way that no inoffensive, antiseptic storybook could.

4. Now turn back and look carefully at the introductory paragraph of Rick's roller coaster speech, and then look at the suggestions for writing strong conclusions. Imagine that Rick has completed the first part of his conclusion by reminding his audience of the major points he made in supporting his thesis statement. He hopes that by now the audience shares some of his enthusiasm. For a strong finish, he might consider one of the following ideas:

- How the **names** of many coasters emphasize their goal of terrifying the rider: Egaphobia, Magnum XL 200, Mind Eraser, Exterminator, Disaster Transport.

- Their remarkable **evolution** from the Gravity Switchback Railroads of 1884 to the tallest, fastest, most complex coasters of today's amusement parks.

- The **variety of features** in contemporary coaster design: inverted cars, corkscrews, knife-edge turns, 180° barrel rolls, speed spirals, and loops—diving, vertical, oblique.

- How the increasing popularity of coasters—67 new ones built in 1998—might connect with the rise of **Extreme Sports**—sky surfing, snow boarding, freestyle skiing, BMX racing, base jumping, bungee jumping, and the like.

- How the roller coaster has become a **symbol** of the quest for ever more intense thrills, and what this says about contemporary American life.

- The **future development** of coasters; what new, fantastic features will designers dream up to terrify the next generation?

- The role of **computer-assisted design tools** in the future; how might they add to the 27 varieties of coasters currently in use throughout the world?

- The matter of **safety**: during the past 11 years there were 11 roller coaster-related fatalities in the United States. Is riding a coaster really "safer than riding a bicycle"?

- The implications of an **apt quotation** such as the following: Charles Lindberg: "A ride on the Cyclone is a greater thrill than flying an airplane at top speed," or the familiar saying, "A carousel is the soul of an amusement park, but a roller coaster is its heart."

Based on these suggestions, try writing the concluding paragraphs of Rick's essay. Then think about how you might apply these ideas to go beyond your thesis statement to bring your own essay to a satisfying close. Does the history of your subject offer some possibilities? Can you predict a future development? Raise a provocative question? Suggest an unresolved problem that is worth pursuing?

Summary

Introduction

- Includes focusing sentences, thesis statement, and method of development.

- Is original; contains nothing borrowed, except as noted.

- Sets the tone, generates interest.

- Avoids the formulaic by including something special—a surprising story, statistic, connection, example, or saying.

Conclusion

- Includes refocusing sentences, reminder of thesis statement, and brief recapitulation.

- Is original; contains nothing borrowed, except as noted.

- Leaves a strong impression.

- Goes beyond the thesis statement by suggesting implications, raising questions, or viewing the topic in a larger context.

- Reflects the introduction.

Chapter 19
Revising and Proofreading

From the time you begin your rough draft until you hand in your paper, the process of revision is continuous. Although it is impossible to list all the possible ways you can improve your writing, this chapter suggests a few questions you should ask. They will help you see where you might want to make some changes. It also includes a checklist and a list of frequently used correction symbols to help you understand your teachers' and classmates' suggestions for improvement. Since many schools and departments have their own rules, be sure to follow local guidelines. When in doubt, ask your teacher.

Question 1.   How can I improve my word choice?

- Have I used dull, trite, childish, and overworked words like very, interesting, thing, involved with, due to the fact, sort of, kind of, big/little, pretty, nice, and beautiful?

- Have I used empty adverbs like hopefully, actually, obviously, certainly, simply, importantly, frankly, arguably, and famously?

- Have I avoided clichés, e.g., last but not least, beat around the bush, light as a feather, level playing field, bottom line, and down the tube?

Question 2.   Have I chosen the best verbs for the job?

- Have I used strong action verbs instead of verbs of being, e.g., <u>crashed</u> instead of <u>is down</u>; <u>participates</u> instead of <u>is in</u>; <u>withdrew</u> instead of <u>has been out of it</u>?

- Have I used active rather than passive verbs, e.g., saying, "I made a mistake" instead of "Mistakes were made"?

Question 3.   Do my sentences show variety in length and structure?

- Do they all have the same boring structure, e.g., simple sentences in subject-verb order, as in "The teacher's dog ate our homework"?

- Are they all the same boring length?

- Are there places where I should try sentence combining, joining sentences to show the relationship of ideas?

- Do any of my sentences sound awkward when I read them aloud?

Question 4. Do I show instead of tell, by providing vivid descriptive details, figurative language, examples, or anecdotes? For example:

Telling	Showing
The teacher was angry.	The teacher's face turned crimson, and she screamed, "Stop, you idiot! Writing on the desk drives me insane."
	The teacher became an erupting volcano.
	The teacher was furious. It reminded me of the time we locked Ms. Gaffney in the gym office, and she had to climb out the window.

Question 5. Have I used transitions—words like however, then, on the other hand, and furthermore—to improve the coherence and flow of my writing?

Question 6. Have I paid attention to the basic rules of expository writing? That is:

- Do my introductory paragraphs include a clear, concise thesis statement and a method of development (MOD)?
- Do my topic sentences connect to my thesis statement?
- Do my body paragraphs provide support for my thesis statement?
- Does my conclusion remind the reader of my thesis statementd then go beyond it in some intriguing way?

Question 7. When using borrowed material, have I provided:

- A lead-in, identifying the speaker or situation?
- An accurate quotation?
- A follow-up, a comment or analysis of the quotation?

Question 8. Have I observed the rules of grammar and usage? Avoiding:

- Run-ons?
- Fragments?
- Misplaced modifiers?
- Passive voice?
- Lack of agreement between subject and verb, pronoun and antecedent?

Question 9. Have I paid attention to mechanics, making sure that my capitalization and punctuation are correct?

Question 10. Have I checked spelling carefully, using a dictionary when in doubt, running a spelling checker, and looking especially for errors that the spelling checker cannot find, e.g., their/there/they're, to/too/two, effect/affect, it's/its, then/than, were/where, and lie/lay?

Keep in mind the message of that widely circulated, anonymous poem that pops up everywhere from Ann Landers's column to various Internet sites, warning you not to rely too heavily on this device:

> I have a spelling checker,
>
> It came with my PC.
>
> It plainly marks four my revue
>
> Miss steaks I cannot sea.
>
> I've run this poem threw it,
>
> I'm sure your pleased too no,
>
> Its letter perfect in it's weigh,
>
> My checker tolled me sew.

Another important aspect of revising and proofreading is learning from your mistakes. It's a good idea to keep an error inventory, noting mistakes you've made in previous writing assignments. Even if you haven't kept an inventory, you should look back over your writing portfolio to make sure that you understand the corrections and suggestions that your teachers and classmates have made so that you can avoid those problems in future assignments. And it's especially important to notice also what you've done well and to build on those strengths.

Checklist for Revising and Proofreading Your Research Paper

Formatting

____ I have used standard, easily readable 12 pt. type and have set margins at one inch all around.

____ I have set the Tab key to indent one-half inch (or five spaces) for each paragraph.

____ My title, centered, is on the top line of the first page of my paper. I have followed the rules below:
- **Do not** write your title all in capital letters.
- **Do not** underline or use quotation marks.
- **Do** capitalize the **first** letter of the first word and the last word and all other words in the title **except for** articles (a, an, the); prepositions (of, in, on, against, between, to, etc.); and coordinating conjunctions (and, but, or, nor, for, so, yet).
- **Do** skip a line between your title and the first line of your essay.

____ I used double-spacing throughout my paper, including long direct quotations and my works cited or references page.

____ I noted my teacher's instructions about the heading, that is, the placement of name, subject, and date. The customary practices include the following: 1) place the heading in the upper right corner of the first page; 2) place the heading in the upper left corner of the first page (MLA); 3) prepare a separate title page, or complete a previously distributed cover sheet, with the essential information:

> Sam Spade
> World History, Per. 3
> January 7, 2021

Mechanics, Usage and Style

____ I have written in a style appropriate to the subject, assignment, and audience. I have avoided contractions, abbreviations, colloquialisms, and slang.

____ After each addition to or revision of my paper, I have run a spelling and grammar check and have corrected misspellings, typos, and other errors, being careful to **save** before checking spelling and also after making corrections. I have proofread the final version carefully myself, and I have persuaded at least one additional human being to proofread as well.

____ I have checked my entire paper for:
- Errors in grammar and usage.

- Consistency of point of view and of verb use: maintaining one tense throughout the essay except where a tense shift is appropriate.
- Use of present tense in discussion of literature and literary criticism.
- Use of third person in literary analysis and expository writing except where a shift to first person is appropriate.
- Errors in punctuation, noting especially that the period comes **after** the parenthetical citation except for long, indented quotations.

____ I have underlined or italicized all titles of books, plays, long poems, periodicals, films, musicals, radio and television programs, compact discs, audiocassettes, works of art, and reference works, whether used in the text or in the documentation of my paper. I have placed quotation marks around the titles of stories, poems, essays, songs, chapters, and the like. When in doubt, I have checked with the authorities on this and other questions about punctuation.

____ After the first reference to an individual, I have used his or her last name only, except where doing so would cause confusion with other family members. I have used the full name again only in my concluding paragraph.

____ Whether writing at home or at school, I have followed all instructions about formatting, pagination, heading, cover sheet, and the like, and I have included my name on the first page or cover sheet, as instructed. I have omitted a slippery plastic cover, knowing that most teachers hate slippery plastic covers.

____ I have read my entire rough draft aloud, at least once, to catch awkwardness, repetition, faulty logic, and the like because I know the ear will catch much that the eye misses.

Documentation and Use of Borrowed Material

____ I have used a variety of sources and have not relied too heavily on one. I have used print sources as well as those on the Internet, and I have evaluated my sources for reliability.

____ There is **no** borrowed material in my paper that is not on my note cards. I can produce all sources if asked. I have avoided plagiarism by paraphrasing thoroughly and by providing accurate documentation, including in-text citations and a works cited or references page

____ I have checked all borrowed material for proper use and accuracy: I have either summarized, paraphrased thoroughly, or used direct quotations correctly, introducing all direct quotations, using quotation marks, and showing omissions with ellipses, that is, ….

____ I have provided the sources for all borrowed material, whether directly or indirectly quoted, whether quoted, paraphrased, or summarized, and I have provided parenthetical citations in the correct form, that is: (Smith 144); (155); (Morgan 44, 117); ("Volcano" 193).

____ I have developed and expanded my borrowed material, not merely stating facts but explaining, commenting, and providing connections. I have not just strung together a number of quotations; I have integrated them into my discussion and have included my own ideas and analysis, in addition to the ideas of others.

____ I have checked my works cited or references page, making sure that:
- It includes all the works mentioned in my paper.
- It includes only the works mentioned.

The entries:

▶ Are alphabetized, not numbered.

▶ Are punctuated and capitalized according to MLA or APA rules.

▶ Correspond to the sources cited in my text.

Structure and Content

____ My thesis paragraph contains focusing sentences, thesis statement, and method of development; my body paragraphs have strong topic sentences and present material that supports my thesis statement.

____ I have used transitions throughout my paper.

____ I have paid attention to all corrections, comments, and questions that my teachers and classmates have provided to help me, and I have tried to improve my paper in the ways suggested.

____ This paper reflects my best effort.

Proofreading and Correction Symbols

Individual teachers, schools, style manuals, and dictionaries all suggest different ways to indicate errors in written work. The notation given here includes symbols that many teachers and students find useful as shorthand to mark errors and suggest improvements. Examples follow the error or writing weakness when appropriate.

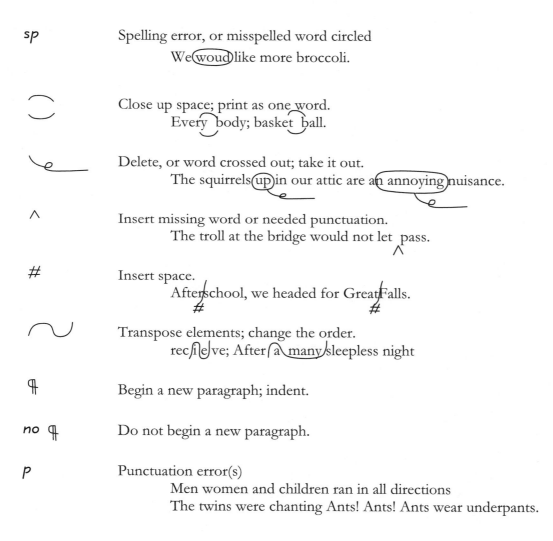

sp   Spelling error, or misspelled word circled

              We woud like more broccoli.

       Close up space; print as one word.

              Every body; basket ball.

       Delete, or word crossed out; take it out.

              The squirrels up in our attic are an annoying nuisance.

∧   Insert missing word or needed punctuation.

              The troll at the bridge would not let pass.

Insert space.

              Afterschool, we headed for GreatFalls.

       Transpose elements; change the order.

              recieve; After a many sleepless night

¶   Begin a new paragraph; indent.

no ¶   Do not begin a new paragraph.

P   Punctuation error(s)

              Men women and children ran in all directions

              The twins were chanting Ants! Ants! Ants wear underpants.

ss		Faulty sentence structure; specific errors may include the following:

frag   Sentence fragment or incomplete sentence; add the missing parts, often the main verb.

> Because our teamwork was superior.
> Under the stairway, where no one had looked.

r-o   Run-on sentence, also called comma splice; two sentences run together with no punctuation or joined only by a comma; provide the correct punctuation.

> ▷ We're planning a party, we've invited everyone.
> ▷ Jane wrote the lyrics, Carlos composed the music.

dm
mm   Dangling or misplaced modifier; rearrange the sentence.

> Racing toward the finish, a pothole made him stumble.
> Samantha saw a dog gnawing a bone on her way to school.

//   Faulty parallel structure; when presenting a series, be consistent in your use of specific parts of speech, infinitives, and verbals.

> We held a bake sale, a car wash, and we sold raffle tickets.
> The club president's duties include planning the program, running the meetings, and to make sure that new members feel welcome.

pv   Passive voice; make your verbs active; give the grammatical subject of the sentence the action.

> Active: The aardvark ate my birthday cake.
> Passive: My birthday cake was eaten by the aardvark.

c, cap, or ≡   Capitalization error(s); use a capital letter.

> In english I'm reading a novel about indians.

lc or /   Use a lower case letter.

> I plan to study Sociology and Basket Weaving in College.

agr   Lack of agreement between subject and verb (s-v) or between pronoun and antecedent (p-a); make both singular, or both plural.

> Neither Matthew nor Hannah know the answer.
> Everyone should open their books to page 17.

shift/t   Shift from one tense to another, e.g., past to present

shift/pov   Shift from one point of view to another, e.g., first person to third. Be consistent in the use of verb tenses and point of view.

ww
Wrong word; word does not have the meaning suggested.
He flaunted the rules until the principal expelled him.
[The writer means **flout**, not **flaunt**].

wc
Weak word choice; tone or level of language inappropriate
A bunch of guys started harassing us kids; the thing about it was, the fight became pretty interesting.

?
Vague or ambiguous; make your meaning clear.

awk
Awkward; clumsy phrasing or sentence structure
Rewrite sentence, striving for grace, balance, and clarity.

gr
Grammatical error
Between you and I, she is a liar and a thief.
When I saw him laying on the floor, I almost died.

log
Faulty logic
It's not true that smoking causes cancer; my grandfather smokes a pack a day and he's 85.
The astronauts saw no angels in outer space, so obviously angels don't exist.

w
Wordiness
The alarm, which I set the night before, went off extremely early at 6 a.m. before the sun came up at dawn.

rep
Needless repetition
In Salinger's novel, Salinger shows many of the problems of adolescents and young people.

red
Redundancy: salty brine; hot water heater; pizza pie

trans
Transition needed; provide transitional words or phrases to link ideas, sentences, paragraphs.

coh
Problems with coherence; paragraph lacks unity and organization; does not hang together. Rethink your focus; re-examine your thesis statement (Th S), topic sentence (TS), and supporting ideas.

lr. or ref.
Indefinite reference
As the creature emerged from the black lagoon, it was silent.
[The reference of <u>it</u> is unclear].

Summary

Revising and Proofreading

To revise and proofread your paper, take a close look at:

- Formatting: type, margins, indentation, spacing, title, and heading.

- Mechanics: grammar, spelling, capitalization, and punctuation.

- Style and usage: word choice, sentence variety and length, and appropriateness of language to specific task.

- Structure: Introduction with focus, thesis statement, and method of development. Body paragraphs with clear topic sentences.

- Transitions throughout.

- Conclusion with restated thesis, recapitulation, and sentences that go beyond.

- Use of borrowed material: paraphrasing, summarizing, and direct quotation.

- Lead-ins and follow-ups for direct quotations; variety of sources.

- Documentation: parenthetical citations, works cited or references.

Chapter 20A
Works Cited
MLA

This final chapter provides the rules and examples that you need to prepare the works cited page for your research project, the last step in a long journey. Providing full information about your sources so that others may find them is an essential aspect of being a responsible researcher. Since the MLA and the APA give quite different specifications, as explained in chapter 1, we provide a separate chapter for each form. **Be sure you check carefully and use the form your teacher requires.**

To prepare your works cited page, take your source cards, check for any errors or omissions, and sort out the cards for the sources that you **actually used** in writing your paper. **Remember that all ideas and information you borrow must be cited and that your works cited must match the parenthetical citations in your text.** Put the unused cards away. Review the information in Step 3 in chapter 9A, pages 51-52, and then proceed as follows.

Step 1.   Arrange cards alphabetically by author.

Do **not** number the entries on your works cited page. Check the model.

Where there is no author, as in unsigned newspaper, magazine, or other articles, use the title of the article, alphabetizing according to the first significant word in the title.

Step 2.   Punctuate carefully.

Underline or italicize book titles, plays, long poems, pamphlets, periodicals (newspapers, magazines, journals), films, radio and television programs, compact discs, audio- and videocassettes, record albums, ballets, operas, and other long musical compositions, paintings, and works of sculpture.

Put quotation marks around the titles of articles, essays, chapters, poems, short stories, and episodes of radio and television programs. Your entries should match the models provided here.

Step 3.   Double check publication information, remembering to shorten publishers' names:

> Harcourt instead of Harcourt Brace
>
> Simon instead of Simon and Schuster
>
> Holt instead of Holt, Rinehart and Winston
>
> Norton instead of W.W. Norton
>
> Scribner's instead of Charles Scribner's Sons
>
> Princeton UP instead of Princeton University Press

When in doubt, check section 7.5 in the <u>MLA Handbook</u>, or ask your teacher.

Step 4.   Capitalize first, last, and all major words in titles, including those following hyphens in compound words. That is, capitalize all words except articles (a, an, the), prepositions (in, on, of, against, between, among, etc.), coordinating conjunctions (and, but, for, or, nor, so, yet), and <u>to</u> in infinitives.

> <u>A Tale of Two Cities</u>
>
> <u>Studies in Classic American Literature</u>
>
> <u>Black Voices: An Anthology of Afro-American Literature</u>
>
> "Ode to a Nightingale" (poem)
>
> "Fitzgerald: The Horror and the Vision of Paradise" (short story)
>
> "The Worms of the Earth against the Lions" (chapter)

Step 5.   Start a new file for your works cited page.

- Begin your works cited at the top of a new page.
- The title Works Cited—no quotation marks, no underline, and not in all CAPS—appears at the center of the top line of the page.
- Double-space the entire works cited page.
- Begin each entry flush with the left margin.
- Indent five spaces or one-half inch after the first line of each entry.
- Use ---. instead of repeating an author's name for the second entry by the same writer.
- Proofread carefully.
- Number your works cited page consecutively with the rest of your paper, that is, if your paper ends on page 7, then your works cited page is page 8.
- For the form of any entries not included on this page, check the examples that follow. The next page is a sample works cited page from Paloma's paper on film and musical versions of <u>The Adventures of Huckleberry Finn</u>. Your works cited page should match this form, regardless of the subject matter of your paper.

Works Cited

Bollinger, Laurel. "Say It, Jim: The Morality of Connection in Adventures of
    Huckleberry Finn." College Literature 29 (2002): 32-53. Literature Resource
    Center. Gale, 2004. White Oak Public Lib., Silver Spring, MD. 8 March 2004
    <http://infotrac.galegroup.com/>.

Cope, Virginia H., ed. Mark Twain's Huckleberry Finn: Text, Illustrations, and
    Early Reviews. Electronic Text Center. Ed. David Seaman. 1995. Alderman
    Lib., U of Virginia. 8 March 2004 <http://etext.lib.virginia.edu/twain/
    huckfinn.html>.

Haupt, Clyde V. Huckleberry Finn on Film: Film and Television Adaptations of
    Mark Twain's Novel, 1920-1993. Jefferson, NC: McFarland, 1994.

Hearn, Michael Patrick, ed. The Annotated Huckleberry Finn: Huckleberry Finn
    (Tom Sawyer's comrade) by Mark Twain [Samuel L. Clemens]. 1885. New
    York: Norton, 2001.

Hill, Dick, narr. The Adventures of Huckleberry Finn: The Classic Collection. By
    Mark Twain. Brilliance Audio, 2001.

Miller, Roger. Big River. Perf. Rene Auberjonois, Patti Cohenour, John Goodman,
    Bob Gunton, Susan Browning, Gordon Connell. Rec. 1985. Decca, 1990.

Murray, Matthew. Rev. of Big River: The Adventures of Huckleberry Finn.
    Talkinbroadway.com. 24 July 2003. 8 March 2004 <http://
    www.talkinbroadway.com/world/BigRiver.html>.

Rich, Frank. "With Huck Finn on Big River." New York Times on the Web
    26 April 1985. 8 March 2004 <http://theater2.nytimes.com/mem/
    theater/treview.html>.

Examples of Works Cited Entries—MLA

Books

A Book by One Author

Pinker, Steven. <u>The Blank Slate: The Modern Denial of Human Nature</u>. New York: Viking, 2002.

Two or More Books by the Same Author

Sontag, Susan. <u>Regarding the Pain of Others</u>. New York: Picador, 2004.

---. <u>Against Interpretation: And Other Essays</u>. New York: Picador, 2001.

A Book by Two Authors

Frum, David, and Richard Perle. <u>An End to Evil: How to Win the War on Terror</u>. New York: Random, 2004.

A Book by Three Authors

Brown, Daniel, Alan W. Scheflin, and D. Corydon Hammond. <u>Memory, Trauma Treatment, and the Law</u>. New York: Norton, 2004.

A Book with Multiple Authors (more than three)

Jolly, Richard, Louis Emmerij, Dharam Ghai, and Frédéric Lapeyer. <u>UN Contributions to Development Thinking and Practice</u>. Bloomington: Indiana UP, 2004.

or

Jolly, Richard, et al. <u>UN Contributions to Development Thinking and Practice</u>. Bloomington: Indiana UP, 2004.

A Book by a Corporate Author

Office for Intellectual Freedom. <u>Intellectual Freedom Manual</u>. 6th ed. Chicago: American Library Association, 2002.

A Work in an Anthology or Compilation (essay, speech, poem, or short story)

DuBois, W. E. B. <u>The Souls of Black Folk</u>. <u>Norton Anthology of African American Literature</u>. Ed. Henry Louis Gates, Jr. and Nellie Y. McKay. New York: Norton, 1996. 613-739.

Tanner, Tony. "Afterthoughts on Don DeLillo's <u>Underworld</u>." Rev. of <u>Underworld</u>, by Don DeLillo. <u>Raritan</u> 17 (1998): 48-71. Rpt. in <u>Contemporary Literary Criticism</u>. Vol. 143. Detroit: Gale, 2001. 206-15.

Williams, Carol T. "Nabokov's Dozen Short Stories: His World in Microcosm." <u>Studies in Short Fiction</u> 12 (1975): 213-22. Rpt. in <u>Twentieth Century American Literature</u>. Ed. Harold Bloom. Vol. 5. New York: Chelsea, 1987. 2807-11.

A Book with an Editor as Author

Lim, Shirley, ed. <u>Asian-American Literature: An Anthology</u>. New York: McGraw, 2000.

An Article in a Reference Work

"Anna Klumpke." <u>Encyclopedia of Lesbian, Gay, Bisexual and Transgendered History in America</u>. Ed. Mark Stein. New York: Scribner's, 2003.

An Unsigned Article in a Reference Work

"Chaos Theory." <u>Columbia Encyclopedia</u>. 6th ed. 2001.

"Existentialism." <u>Encyclopedia Britannica</u>. 2001 ed.

An Introduction, Preface, Foreword, or Afterword

Koop, C. Everett. Foreward. <u>Dr. Folkman's War: Angiogenesis and the Struggle to Defeat Cancer</u>. By Robert Cooke. New York: Random, 2001.

An Anonymous Book

<u>New York Public Library Desk Reference</u>. 4th ed. New York: Hyperion, 2002.

Holy Bible. Authorized King James Version. London: Collins, 1949.

A Translation

Pinsky, Robert, trans. <u>The Inferno of Dante</u>. Bilingual ed. New York: Noonday, 1996.

A Pamphlet

Rosenthal, M. L. <u>Randall Jarrell</u>. Pamphlets on American Writers no. 103. Minneapolis: U of Minnesota P, 1972.

A Government Publication

<u>Long Passage to Korea: Black Sailors and the Integration of the United States Navy</u>. Washington: GPO, 2003. [Government Printing Office]

A Multivolume Work

Sadie, Stanley, and John Tyrrell, eds. <u>The New Grove Dictionary of Music and Musicians</u>. 2nd ed. 29 vols. London: Macmillan, 2001.

Periodicals

An Article in a Scholarly Journal

Ganem, Don, and Alfred M. Prince. "Hepatitis B Virus Infection—Natural History and Consequences." <u>New England Journal of Medicine</u> 350 (2004): 1118-29.

Grcic, Joseph. "Truth in Ethics: A Pragmatic Approach." <u>Prima-Philosophia</u> 16.1 (2003): 43-59.

An Article in a Magazine

Crawford, Craig. "Kerry's Vietnam War Record Draws Supporters from Both Sides." <u>CQ Weekly</u> (<u>Congressional Quarterly</u>) 21 Feb 2004: 464-65.

Saul, John Ralston. "The Collapse of Globalism and the Rebirth of Nationalism." <u>Harpers</u> Mar. 2004: 33-43.

An Unsigned Magazine Article

"Vietnamese Americans: Lessons in American History." <u>Teaching Tolerance</u> Spring 2004: 31-35.

A Document

Truman, Harry S. "The Recall of General Douglas MacArthur." <u>Documents of American History since 1898</u>. Ed. Henry Steele Commager. Englewood Cliffs: Prentice, 1973. 67-69.

An Article in a Newspaper

DePalma, Anthony. "Toxic Dumping Ground Looks to Spread the Pain." <u>New York Times</u> 10 Mar. 2004, New England ed.: A23. [Monday through Saturday]

Burns, John F. "The Road Ahead May Be Even Rougher." <u>New York Times</u> 7 Mar. 2004, New England ed., sec. 4:1. [Sunday]

An Unsigned Article in a Newspaper

"Air-Safety Standards Stay Elusive." <u>Wall Street Journal</u> 10 Mar. 2004: 14.

An Editorial in a Newspaper

"Why Discriminate?" Editorial. <u>Boston Globe</u> 10 Mar. 2004: A22.

A Letter to the Editor in a Newspaper

Davar, Tamina. Letter. <u>Christian Science Monitor</u> 9 Mar. 2004: 8.

A Review

Acocella, Joan. "No Bloody Toe Shoes." Rev. of <u>The Company</u>. Dir. Robert Altman. Screenplay by Barbara Turner. <u>New York Review of Books</u> 26 Feb. 2004: 7-8.

Kirsch, A. "The Radical Strangeness of Being." Rev. of <u>The Metaphysician in the Dark</u>, by Charles Simic. <u>Times Literary Supplement</u> 5 Mar. 2004: 11.

Other Sources

A Television or Radio Program

"The Elegant Universe." <u>Nova</u>. PBS. WGBH, Boston. 9 Mar. 2004.

A Sound Recording

Bernstein, Leonard. <u>Candide</u>. Lyrics by Richard Wilbur. Orch. London Symphony. Perf. London Symphony Chorus. Deutsche Grammophon, 1991.

Muhaiyaddeen, M. R. <u>Bawa. Islam and World Peace: Explanations of a Sufi</u>. Read by M.E. Willis. Audiocassette. Audio Literature, 2002.

A Film, Filmstrip, Slide Program, or Video Recording

Chaplin, Charles, dir. <u>City Lights</u>. Perf. Chaplin and Virginia Cherrill. 1931. Chaplin Collection, vol. 2. DVD. Warner, 2004.

A Performance

<u>King Lear</u>. By William Shakespeare. Dir. Jonathan Miller. Perf. Christopher Plummer. Vivian Beaumont Theater, Lincoln Center, New York. 10 Apr. 2004.

A Published Musical Composition

Joplin, Scott. <u>Treemonisha</u>. Vocal Score. New York: Dover, 2001.

A Work of Art

Brueghel, Pieter. <u>Landscape with the Fall of Icarus</u>. Musées Royaux des Beaux-Arts, Brussels.

A Letter

Ondaatje, Michael. Letter to the author. 14 Jan. 2003.

An Interview

Reagan, Ronald. Telephone interview. 8 Aug. 1986.

Sharpton, Al. Personal interview. 30 Sept. 2004.

A Map or Chart

<u>Vermont</u>. Map. Montpelier: Vermont Attractions Assoc., 2003.

A Lecture, Speech, Address

Bush, George W. State of the Union Address. United States Congress, Washington.

30 Jan. 2004.

Electronic Sources

Although the rules for documenting electronic sources have undergone a number of changes since the advent of the Internet, the MLA has established clear rules for these references. Electronic sources are not as stable as their print counterparts, so references to electronic works require more information than print citations. The citation for an electronic publication may include five divisions: author's name, document title, and information about print publication, electronic publication, and access. **Where complete information is not available, provide as much as you can find.**

The URL (uniform resource locator) should be provided in citations of online works, along with other information that will help readers to locate the source easily. Place the URL immediately after the date of access at the end of the citation, separated by a space but with no punctuation preceding it. Enclose the URL in angle brackets (< >) with a period following the closing bracket. Divide an URL only after a slash (/). Give the complete address except where the URL for a specific document in a database is so long and complicated that transcription errors are probable. In such cases, give the URL of the site's search page or home page. To guide the reader to the specific document, place the word Path after the URL, followed by a colon, and then provide the links, separated by semicolons, as in the example below.

"The History of Women's Suffrage in America." <u>History Channel.com</u>. 2004. History

Channel. 18 Mar. 2004 <http://www.historychannel.com/>. Path: Women's History;

Women's Suffrage.

> **Note:**
>
> URLs are frequently omitted when material is obtained from a library or personal subscription service. The <u>MLA Handbook</u> lists the following 15 items that citations for electronic sources may include if the information is available:

1. Name of author, editor, compiler, or translator
2. Title of article, poem, short story, or the like (in quotation marks)
3. Title of a book (underlined)
4. Name of editor, compiler, or translator, if not cited earlier
5. Publication information for print version

6. Title of Internet site (scholarly project, database, online periodical, professional site, underlined)

7. Name of editor of site

8. Version number of source or volume number of journal

9. Date of electronic posting or latest update

10. For a work from a subscription service, name of service and geographic location of subscriber

11. For posting to discussion list or forum, name of list or forum

12. Number range or total number of pages, paragraphs, or other sections

13. Name of institution or organization sponsoring the site

14. Date when researcher accessed the source

15. URL of the source, search page, or home page

An Online Scholarly Project, Information Database, Journal, or Professional Site

Include the following information: title of project or database, underlined; name of editor; publication information, including version number, date or latest update; name of sponsoring institution or organization; date of access, URL.

Banned Books Online. Ed. John Mark Ockerbloom. 1993-2003. Online Books Page, U of
   Pennsylvania. 18 Mar. 2004 <http://onlinebooks.library.upenn.edu/banned-
   books.html>.

The Little Red Riding Hood Project. Ed. Michael N. Salda. Vers. 1.0. Dec. 1995. De
   Grummond Children's Literature Research Collection, U of Southern Mississippi.
   18 Mar. 2004 <http://www.usm.edu/english/fairytales/lrrh/lrrhhome.htm>.

A Document within a Scholarly Project or Information Database

To cite an article, poem, short story, or similar document, include the following: author's name; title of the work, in quotation marks; information about print publication; information about electronic publication; date of access; URL. For works from a subscription service, e.g., EBSCO, DIALOG, SIRS, or Gale, list the name of the subscribing library, city, and state, abbreviated, before the access date.

"Carnegie, Andrew." Encyclopedia Britannica Online. Vers. 99.1. Encyclopedia Britannica.
   White Oak Public Lib., Silver Spring, MD. 18 Mar. 2004 <http://www.eb.com>.

Feeney, Kathleen. "Bloomer, Amelia Jenks." American National Biography Online.
   American Council of Learned Societies and Oxford UP. Feb. 2000. Walt Whitman
   High School Lib., Bethesda, MD. 18 Mar. 2004 <http://www.anb.org/>.

Gilman, Charlotte Perkins. "The Yellow Wallpaper." Boston: Maynard Small, 1899. <u>Electronic Text Center</u>. Ed. David Seaman. 1997. Alderman Lib., U of Virginia. 18 Mar. 2004 <http://etext.lib.virginia.edu/subjects/Women-Writers.html>.

Kirsch, Adam. "Unphantasmal Peace." [criticism of Derek Walcott] <u>New Republic</u> 15 Dec. 1997: 42. <u>Contemporary Literary Criticism Select</u>. <u>InfoTrac</u>. Gale. Brooks Memorial Lib., Brattleboro, VT. 18 Mar. 2004 <http://www.galenet.galegroup.com/>.

"Powell, Colin." <u>Encyclopedia Britannica</u>. 2004. Encyclopedia Britannica Premium Service. 18 Mar. 2004 <http://www.britannica.com/>.

Rayhanova, Baian. "Mythological and Folkloristic Motifs in Syrian Prose: The Short Stories of Zakariyyā Tāmir." <u>Journal of Arabic and Islamic Studies</u>. 5 (2003): 1-12. <u>Infomine</u>. U of California. 19 Mar. 2004 <http://www.uib.no/jais/content5.html>.

"Trying to Get Their Own Back: Iraq's Kurds." <u>Economist</u> 31 Jan. 2004: 52. <u>ProQuest</u>. Montgomery Blair High School Lib., Silver Spring, MD. 19 Mar. 2004 <http://proquest.umi.com/login>.

"John Updike." <u>Contemporary Authors</u>. 2004. <u>InfoTrac</u>. Gale. Brooks Memorial Library, Brattleboro, VT. 18 Mar. 2004 <http://www.galenet.galegroup.com/>.

Watson, Paul. "U.S. Abuses in Afghanistan Are Alleged." <u>Los Angeles Times</u> 8 Mar. 2004. <u>SIRS Researcher</u>. Winston Churchill High School Lib., Bethesda, MD. 18 Mar. 2004 <http://sks.sirs.com>.

An Online Book Not within a Scholarly Project or Information Database

Include the following information: author's name or name of editor, compiler, or translator; title; print publication information, including place of publication, publisher, and date of original print version, if available; electronic publication information; access date and URL.

Shakespeare, William. <u>The Merchant of Venice</u>. <u>The Complete Works of William Shakespeare</u>. The Tech, MIT. Modified 1999. 18 Mar. 2004 <http://the-tech.mit.edu/>. Path: Works of Shakespeare; The Merchant of Venice.

Twain, Mark. <u>The Adventures of Huckleberry Finn</u>. 1885. <u>Project Gutenberg</u>. 1993. 20 Mar. 2004 <http://www.gutenberg.net/dirs/7/76/76-h/p1.htm#c1>.

Part of an Online Book

When citing part of an online book, place the title of the part cited between the author's name and the title of the book. Enclose the title of a poem, essay, or short story in quotation marks. Include access date and URL for the specific part of the book being cited.

Dickinson, Emily. "I like to see it lap the miles." <u>Complete Poems of Emily Dickinson</u>. Boston: Little, 1924. <u>Bartleby.com: Great Books Online</u>. Ed. Steven van Leeuwen. 2000. 20 Mar. 2004 <http://www.bartleby.com/113/1043>.

Hawthorne, Nathaniel. "The Minister's Black Veil." <u>Twice-Told Tales</u>. Ed. George Parsons Lathrop. Boston: Houghton, 1883. Eldritch Press. 20 Mar. 2004 <http://eldritchpress.org/nh/mbv.html>.

Milton, John. "Areopagitica: A Speech for the Liberty of Unlicensed Printing." 1643. <u>Harvard Classics</u>. Ed. Charles W. Eliot. New York: Collier, 1909-14: 195-236. Universal Library. Carnegie Mellon U. 20 Mar. 2004. <http://www.ulib.org/html/index.html>.

Poe, Edgar Allan. "The Cask of Amontillado." <u>The Complete Works of Edgar Allan Poe</u>. 1846. EServer. Iowa State U. 20 Mar. 2004 <http://eserver.org/books/poe/cask_of_amontillado.html>.

An Online Government Publication

National Institute on Alcohol Abuse and Alcoholism. National Institutes of Health. <u>The Genetics of Alcoholism</u>. Alcohol Alert no. 60. July 2003. 20 Mar. 2004 <http://www.niaaa.nih.gov/publications/aa60.htm>.

An Article in an Online Periodical (newspaper, magazine, or scholarly journal)

Include the following information: author's name; title, in quotation marks; name of periodical, underlined; volume or issue number; date; range or total number of pages or paragraphs, if numbered; access date; URL.

An Article in a Scholarly Journal:

Hershock, Peter D. "From Vulnerability to Virtuosity: Buddhist Reflections on Responding to Terrorism and Tragedy." <u>Journal of Buddhist Ethics</u> 10 (2003). <u>BUBL Link</u> <http://bubl.ac.uk/link/>. Path: Humanities/Moral Philosophy/Journal of Buddhist Ethics.

Krstic, Igor. "Rethinking Serbia: A Psychoanalytic Reading of Modern Serbian History and Identity through Popular Culture." <u>Other Voices: The (e)Journal of Cultural Criticism</u> 2.2 (2002). 21 Mar. 2004 <http://www.othervoices.org/2.2/krstic/index.html>.

A Newspaper Article

Dreifus, Claudia. "Defying Irreversibility in Spinal Cord Injuries." <u>New York Times on the Web</u> 16 Mar. 2004. 23 Mar. 2004 <http://www.nytimes.com/2004/03/16/science/6CONV.html>.

Gugliotta, Guy. "In Hot Pursuit of Comet to Learn Its Secrets." <u>Washington Post</u> 22 Mar. 2004. 22 Mar. 2004 <http://www.washingtonpost.com/wp-dyn/articles/A13494-2004Mar21.html>

"Liberty or a Lid for Kosovo?" Editorial. <u>Christian Science Monitor</u> 22 Mar. 2004. 22 Mar. 2004 <http://www.csmonitor.com/2004/0322/p08s02-comv.html>.

Triplett, William. "The Search for Extraterrestrials." <u>CQ Researcher Online</u>.14.9 (2004). Poolesville High School Lib., Poolesville, MD. 22 Mar. 2004 <http://library.cqpress.com/cqresearcher>.

A Magazine Article or Review

Edelstein, David. "Forget Me Not." Rev. of <u>Eternal Sunshine of the Spotless Mind</u>. <u>Slate</u> 18 Mar. 2004. 22 Mar. 2004 <http://slate.msn.com/id/2097362>.

Fallows, James. "The Fifty-first State?" <u>Atlantic Online</u> Nov. 2002: 53-64. 22 Mar. 2004 <http://www.theatlantic.com/issues/2002/11/fallows.htm>.

A Serialized Article:

Zehr, Mary Ann. "Close to Home." <u>Education Week on the Web</u> 10 Mar. 2004. Pt. 3 of a series, Brown at 50: The Promise Unfulfilled, begun 21 Jan. 2004. 22 Mar. 2004 <http://www.edweek.org/sreports/special_reports_article.cfm?slug=brown.htm>.

An Anonymous Article:

"Digital Photography: What's New? What's Ahead" <u>ConsumerReports.org</u>. Mar. 2004. 5 Apr. 2004 <http://www.consumerreports.org/>. Path: Electronics & Computers; Digital Cameras, Camcorders & Photography Guide.

<u>CD-ROM Programs</u>

For nonperiodical publications, include the following information: author's name or name of editor, compiler, or translator; title, underlined; publication medium, that is, CD-ROM, diskette, or magnetic tape; edition or version; place of publication, publisher, date.

If you cite only part of the work, state which part. If the part is a book-length work, then underline the title. If the part is a shorter work, such as an article, essay, poem, or short story, enclose the title in quotation marks.

For periodical publications, in addition to the above information, include the title of the database, underlined; name of the vendor; and electronic publication date.

For a Nonperiodical Publication:

Abrams, Harry R. <u>The Mystery of Magritte</u>. CD-ROM. Brussels, Belgium: Virtuo, 1997.

"Pandora." <u>Oxford English Dictionary</u>. 2nd ed. CD-ROM. Oxford: Oxford UP, 1992.

"Zionism." <u>Encyclopaedia Judaica</u>. CD-ROM. Vers. 1.0. Jerusalem, Israel, 1997.

For a Periodically Published Datebase on CD-ROM:

"Clinton, Bill." <u>Current Biography Yearbook</u>, 1994. Abstract. <u>Wilson Biographies</u>. CD-ROM. Wilson, 2000.

<u>Dance on Disc: The Complete Catalog of the Dance Collection of the New York Public Library on CD-ROM</u>. CD-ROM. Vers. 1.2. Boston: Hall, 2003.

Roberts, Leslie. "Acid Rain: Forgotten, Not Gone." <u>U.S. News and World Report</u> 1 Nov. 1999: 70. <u>SIRS Researcher Mandarin</u>. CD-ROM. ProQuest, 2001.

"Yatkar-I-Zariran" [Memoirs of Zarir]. "Zoroastrianism." <u>Internet Sacred Text Archive</u>. Ed. J. B. Hare. CD-ROM. Vers. 3. sacred-texts.com, 2003.

Other Electronic Sources

In general, to document other electronic sources, follow the recommendations for citing miscellaneous print and nonprint sources (television or radio program, sound recording, film or video recording, work of art, etc.), modifying the guidelines as appropriate.

A Radio or Television Program

"Andrew Carnegie: Rags to Riches Timeline." <u>The Richest Man in the World: Andrew Carnegie</u>. <u>American Experience</u>. PBSonline/WGBH, Boston. Updated 1999. 24 Mar. 2004 <http://www.pbs.org/wgbh/amex/carnegie/timeline/f_timeline.html>.

"Meltdown at Three Mile Island." <u>American Experience</u>. 5 Apr. 2004. PBSonline/WGBH. Transcript. 10 Apr. 2004 <http://www.pbs.org/wgbh/amex/three/filmmore/transcript/index.html>.

"The Second Intifada and the Death of Oslo." Part 7 of a series The Mideast: A Century of Conflict, begun 30 Sep. 2002. Transcript 8 Oct. 2002. 24 Mar. 2004

<http://www.npr.org/news/specials/mideast/index/history/transcripts/
7th-part.100802.2_nd-intifada.html>.

A Sound Recording or Sound Clip

Cohen, Ed, Elizabeth Richmond-Garza, and John Paul Requelme. "Portraits of Oscar
Wilde." <u>What's the Word?</u> 2002. <u>Modern Language Association</u>. 18 July 2003. MLA.
26 Mar. 2004 <http://www.mla.org/>. Path: MLA program; Browse Participants and
Listen; 2002 Program Topics.

Peoples, Melanie. "The Heavenly Appeal of Moon Pies." <u>Morning Edition</u>. 25 Sep. 2003.
National Public Radio. 6 Apr. 2004 <http://www.npr.org/>. Path: All Programs
A-Z; Morning Edition.

A Film or Film Clip

Blackmun, Harry A. Video Tape 1, Session 1, of The Harry A. Blackmun Oral History
Project. 6 July 1994. Library of Congress Research Centers. 9 Mar. 2004. 9 Apr. 2004
<http://memory.loc.gov/cocoon/blackmun-public/series.html?ID=D10>.

"Visual Arts' Coco Fusco Examines Images of Race and Identity in Photography." Prod.
no.160. 4 Feb. 2004. 27 Mar 2004
<http://www.columbia.edu/cu/news/media/04/cocoFusco/index.html>.

A Painting, Sculpture, or Photograph

Fuseli, Henry. <u>Lady Macbeth.</u> 1784. Louvre, Paris, France. WebMuseum, Paris. Ed. Nicolas
Pioch. Updated 14 July 2002. 27 Mar. 2004
<http://www.ibiblio.org/wm/paint/auth/fuseli/macbeth.jpg>.

Giacometti, Alberto. <u>Tall Woman II</u>. 1960. Museum of Mod. Art Exhibition, New York,
11 Oct. 2001-8 Jan. 2002. 27 Mar. 2004
<http://www.moma.org/exhibitions/2001/giacometti>.

An Interview

McGovern, Ray. "The Skeptical Spy." Interview with Michael Robbins. <u>Mother Jones</u>
10 Mar. 2004 <http://www.motherjones.com/news/qa/2004/03/03_400.html>.

A Map

"Burlington, Vermont." Map. <u>U. S. Gazetteer</u>. U. S. Census Bureau. 27 Mar. 2004
<http://factfinder.census.gov/servlet>. Path: Maps and Geography; Reference Maps.

A Cartoon

Trudeau, Garry. "Bull Tales." Comic strip. <u>Yale Daily News</u>. 1968. 26 Mar. 2004

    <http://www.doonesbury.com/strip/retro/yale/yale83.html>.

An E-Mail

Include the name of the writer; title of the message, if any, taken from the subject line and enclosed in quotation marks; a description of the message that includes the recipient (e.g., "E-mail to the author"); and the date of the message.

Perkins, Seth. "Re: Your campaign for the presidency." E-mail to Ralph Nader.

    15 Mar. 2004.

Walsh, Samantha. E-mail to the author. 18 Jan. 2004.

An Online Posting

Rohan, Michael Scott. "Re: Tolkien and Wagner Fans." Online posting. 15 Mar. 2004.

    27 Mar. 2004 <http://groups.google.com/groups/>. Path: humanities; music;

    composers; wagner.

Vergese, J., et al. "Leisure Activities and the Risk of Dementia in the Elderly." Online

    posting. 20 June 2003. Abstract. <u>Health News Bulletins</u>. [PMID 12815136].

    Alternative Health News Online. 28 Mar. 2004 <http://www.altmedicine.com/>.

Summary

MLA Works Cited

To prepare your works cited page:

- Arrange your source cards in alphabetical order and list your entries in that order.

- Observe MLA rules for formatting, capitalization, punctuation, abbreviations, and order for each entry.

- Follow the rules for each type of entry, e.g., book, article, database, etc.

- Make sure that your works cited entries correspond to your parenthetical citations.

- Double space throughout.

- Check all entries for accuracy and completeness of information and for correctness of form.

Chapter 20B
References APA

This final chapter provides the rules and examples needed to prepare the references page for your research project, the last step in a long journey. Chapter 20A gives the MLA specifications; this chapter does the same for those who prefer the APA format. **Be sure you check carefully and use the form your teacher requires.** Because the APA <u>Manual,</u> cited in chapter 1, is designed for professional researchers as well as for students, it includes many details and distinctions that go beyond what most high school students need. We have therefore omitted these details and present here only a shortened version of the APA rules. Most libraries, including school media centers, have a copy of the <u>Publication Manual of the American Psychological Association</u> (5th ed.), and you should consult it if necessary.

To follow APA guidelines, you list on a page headed References the works you cited in your research project. To start, take your source cards, check for any errors or omissions, and sort out the cards for the sources that you <u>actually used</u> in writing your paper. **Remember that all ideas and information you borrow must be cited and that your references must match the parenthetical citations in your text.** Put the unused cards away. Review the information in Step 3 in chapter 9B, pp. **57-58**, and then proceed as follows.

Step 1.   Arrange cards alphabetically by author.

             Where there is no author, as in unsigned newspaper, magazine, or other articles, use the title of the article and alphabetize according to the first significant word in the title. Alphabetize group authors by the first significant word of the name, as in American Psychological Association.

Step 2.   Punctuate carefully.

- Abbreviations such as chap., Rev. ed., p. (pp.), and vols. are acceptable.

- Italicize (or underline) titles of the following: periodicals, e.g., journals, magazines, newspapers, newsletters, etc.; books, reports, brochures, monographs, manuals, and audiovisual media.

- Do not use quotation marks around chapters in books or titles of articles in journals, books, or magazines. Your entries should match the models provided in this chapter.

- Double check publication information. Provide full names for publishers:

                 Harcourt Brace
                 Prentice-Hall

> Pergamon Press
> Little, Brown
> Harvard University Press
> Basic Books

Step 3.   Capitalize titles according to these rules:

- For an **article, chapter, or book**, capitalize the first word only of title and subtitle, and any proper names.

- For the name of a **magazine or newspaper**, capitalize all words except articles (a, an, the), prepositions (in, on, of, between, among, etc.), and coordinating conjunctions (and, but, or, nor, so, for, yet). But capitalize the article if it is the first word of the title, as in <u>The Editorial Eye</u>.

Examples:

Codd, R. T., & Cohen, B. N. (2003). Predicting college student intention to seek

    help for alcohol abuse. <u>Journal of Social and Clinical Psychology, 22,</u> 168-191.

Bersoff, D. N. (2003). <u>Ethical conflicts in psychology</u> (3rd ed.). Washington, DC:

    American Psychological Association.

Weiner, I. B. (Ed.). (2003). <u>Handbook of psychology</u> (Vols. 1-12). Hoboken, NJ:

    Wiley.

Strubbe, J. H., & Woods, S. C. (2004). The timing of meals. <u>Psychological Review,</u>

    <u>111,</u> 128-141.

Step 4.   Start a new file for your reference list, and start at the top of the page.

- The word References—no quotation marks, no underline, and not in all CAPS—appears at the center of the top line of the page.

- Double-space the entire references page.

- Start each entry at the left margin. Indent subsequent lines five spaces.

- List several works by the same author chronologically. Repeat the author's name.

- Proofread carefully.

- Number your references page consecutively with the rest of your paper. If your paper ends on page 7, then your references page is page 8.

- For the form of any entries not included under Step 3, check the examples that follow. The next page is a sample references page. Your references page should match it in form.

References

Brown, L. M., Shiang, J., & Bongar, B. (2003). Crisis intervention. In I. B. Weiner (Series Ed.), & G. Stricker & T. A. Wideger (Vol. Eds.), Handbook of psychology: Vol. 8. Clinical psychology (pp. 431- 451). Hoboken, NJ: Wiley.

Lazear, E. P. (2004). The Peter principle: A theory of decline. Journal of Political Economy, 112(Suppl.1), S141-163.

Montrose, V. T., Harris, W. E., & Moore, P. J. (2004). Sexual conflict and cooperation under naturally occurring male enforced monogamy. Journal of Evolutionary Biology, 17, 443-452.

Pervin, L. A., & John, O. (Eds.) (1999). Handbook of personality: Theory and research. (2nd ed.). New York: Guilford Press.

Rayler, N., & Oei, T. P. (2004). Role of culture in gambling and problem gambling. Clinical Psychology Review, 23, 1087-1114.

Shamdasani, S. (2003). Jung and the making of modern psychology: The dream of science. Cambridge, England: Cambridge University Press.

Shaw, B., Kraus, N., Chatters, L. M., Connell, C. M., & Ingersoll-Dayton, B. (2004). Emotional support from parents early in life, aging, and health [Electronic version]. Psychology and Aging, 18, 4-12. Retrieved March 29, 2004, from http://www.apa.org/journals/pag/press_releases/ march_2004/pag1914.html

Swan, S., & Andrews, B. (2003). The relationship between shame, eating disorders and disclosure in treatment. British Journal of Clinical Psychology, 42, 367-378.

Tversky, A., & Gilovich, T. (2004). The cold facts about the "Hot Hand" in basketball. In Shafir, E. (Ed.), Preference, belief, and similarity (pp. 257-265). Cambridge: MIT Press. (Reprinted from Chance, 2, 1989, pp.16-21).

Examples of Reference List Entries–APA

Periodicals

Journal article, one author

Pager, D. (2003). The mark of a criminal record. <u>American Journal of Sociology, 108</u>, 937-975.

Journal article, two authors

Ossmann, J. M., & Mulligan, N. W. (2003). Inhibition and attention deficit hyperactivity disorder in adults. <u>American Journal of Psychology, 116(1)</u>, 35-50.

Journal article, three to six authors

Antonuccio, D. O., Danton, W. G., & McClanahan, T. M. (2003). Psychology in the prescription era: Building a firewall between marketing and science. <u>American Psychologist, 5</u>, 1028-1043.

Journal article, more than six authors

Wittenbaum, G. M., Hollingshead, A. B., Paulus, P. B., Hirokawa, R. Y., Ancona, D. C., Peterson, R. S., et al. (2004). The functional perspective as a lens for understanding groups. <u>Small Group Research, 35(1)</u>, 17-43.

Magazine article

Bahrani, Z. (2004, March). Lawless in Mesopotamia. <u>Natural History, 113</u>, 44-49.

Magazine article, no author

The top 10 consumer stories to watch for in 2004. (2004, January). <u>Consumer Research, 87</u>, 26-29.

Newsletter article, no author

Managing historic bridges in Arkansas. (2003, Spring). <u>Society for Industrial Archeology Newsletter, 32</u>, 14-15.

Daily newspaper article

DePalma, A. (2004, March 10). Toxic dumping ground looks to spread the pain. <u>New York Times</u>, p. A23.

Daily newspaper article, no author

Air-safety standards stay elusive. (2004, March 10). <u>Wall Street Journal</u>, p. 14.

Daily newspaper, discontinuous pages

Weiss, J. (2004, March 27). Ads indicative of emotions in marriage debate. <u>Boston Globe</u>, pp. B1, B7.

Weekly or bi-weekly newspaper article, letter to the editor

Schlesinger, Arthur, Jr. (2004, April 8). Disgrace at Guantanamo [Letter to the editor]. <u>New York Review of Books</u>, p. 85.

Monograph

Brainerd, C. J., Reyna, V. F., Howe, M. L., & Kingman, J. (1990). The development of forgetting and reminiscence. <u>Monograph of the Society for Child Research, 55</u> (3-4, Serial No. 222).

Abstract

Blum, H. P. (2004). The wise baby and the wild analyst. <u>Psychoanalytic Psychology, 21</u>. Abstract retrieved March 31, 2004, from PsycARTICLES.

Kopala, L. C., Good, K. P., Koczapski, A. B., & Honer, W. G. (1998). Olfactory deficits in patients with schizophrenia and severe polydipsia. <u>Biological Psychiatry, 43</u>, 497-502. Abstract retrieved March 31, 2004, from ScienceDirect.

Wheatstone, C. (1851). Note relating to M. Foucault's new mechanical proof of the rotation of the earth. <u>Abstracts of the Papers Communicated to the Royal Society of London, 6</u>, 65-68. Abstract retrieved April 1, 2004, from JSTOR.

Non-English journal article, title translated into English

Hong-Quan, L., & Lohoue, N. (2003) Estimations L^ p des solutions de l'equation des ondes sur certains variétés conique [L^p estimates for solutions of the wave equation on certain conical varieties]. <u>Transactions of the American Mathematical Society, 355</u>, 689-711.

Books, Brochures, and Book Chapters

An entire book

Warner, M. (1998). <u>No go the bogeyman: Scaring, lulling, and making mock</u>. New York: Farrar, Straus and Giroux.

Book with multiple authors

Gardner, R. A., & Gardner, B. T. (1998). <u>The structure of learning: From sign stimuli to sign language</u>. Mahwah, NJ: Earlbaum.

Book or brochure with a group author (government agency) as publisher

Committee for Children. (1996). Talking about touching: Personal safety curriculum for preschool/kindergarten. Seattle, WA: Author.

Article or chapter in an edited book

Batsell, W. R., Jr. (2003). Olfaction: Recent advances in learning about odors. In F. S. Davis (Ed.), Handbook of methods in experimental psychology (pp. 299-322). Malden, MA: Blackwell.

Grisso, T., and Appelbaum, P. S. (2003). Is it unethical to offer predictions of future violence? In D. N. Bersoff (Ed.), Ethical conflicts in psychology (3rd ed., pp. 499-505). Washington, DC: American Psychological Association.

Entry in an encyclopedia or dictionary

Rook, K. S. (2000). Loneliness. In A. E. Kazdin (Ed.), Encyclopedia of psychology (Vol. 5, pp. 73-76). New York: Oxford University Press.

Shun, K.-L. (2003). Moral psychology. In A. S. Cua (Ed.), The encyclopedia of Chinese philosophy. (475-479). New York: Routledge.

English translation of a book

Althusser, L. (1996). Writings on psychoanalysis. Corpet, O. & Matheron, F., (Eds.) (J. Mehlman, Trans.). New York: Columbia University Press.

Technical and Research Reports

American Physical Society. (in press). Report of the American Physical Society study group on boost-phase intercept systems for national missile defense. Suppl. to Reviews of Modern Physics.

National Institute of Justice. (2003, September). Eyewitness evidence: A trainer's manual for law enforcement. Special report by Technical Working Group for Eyewitness Evidence (NCJ Publication 188678). Washington, DC: Author.

National Institute of Mental Health. (1998). Genetics and mental disorders. Report of the NIMH's Genetics Workgroup (NIMH Publication 98-4268). Rockville, MD: Author.

United Nations. (1995, August). World urbanization prospects: The 1994 revision: Estimates and projections of urban and rural populations and of urban agglomerations. New York: Author.

Regularly published proceedings of meetings

Manson, N. C. (2003). Freud's own blend: Functional analysis, ideographic explanation, and the extension of ordinary psychology. Proceedings of the Aristotelian Society, NS, 103, 179-195.

Unpublished paper presented at a meeting

Baker, C. H. (2004, February 21). An existentialist take on American foreign policy. Paper presented at a meeting of the Washington Philosophy Club, Washington, DC.

Mahadevan, J. (2004, April 2). Conceptions of power influencing intercultural communication: The Southeast Asian perspective. Paper presented to the 2004 Congress of the Society for Intercultural Education, Training and Research, Berlin, Germany.

Review of a book

Pryce-Jones, D. (2000, March 5). Byzantine tragedy [Review of the book Stalinism for all seasons]. Times Literary Supplement, no. 5266, p. 7.

Review of a motion picture

Wills, G. (2004, April 8). God in the hands of angry sinners [Review of the motion picture The Passion of the Christ]. New York Review, 51, pp. 68-74.

Audiovisual Media

Motion picture or videocassette

American Psychological Association (Producer). (2002). Reclaiming hope in a changing world [videocassette]. (Available from the American Psychological Association, 750 First Street, NE, Washington, DC 20002-4242)

Stantic, L. (Producer), & Martel, L. (Director). (2001). La cienaga (The swamp) [Motion picture]. Argentina: Cuatro Cabezas Films.

Wiedlinger, T. (Writer/Director). (2001). Boys will be men: A documentary about growing up male in America [videocassette]. Reading, PA: Bullfrog films.

Television broadcast

Chapman, P. (Producer). (2003, December 14). The road from Coorain [Television broadcast]. Masterpiece Theater. Public Broadcasting Service. Boston: WGBH.

Television series

> Grubin, D. (Producer). (2002). <u>The secret life of the brain</u> [Television series]. New York: WNET.

Music recording

> Bernstein, L. (1991). The best of all possible worlds [Recorded by London Symphony Orchestra and Chorus]. On <u>Candide</u> [CD]. New York: Polygram Music.

Audio recording

> Markos, L. (Speaker). (2000). Structuralism—Saussure and Levi-Straus. Part 6, lecture 72 of <u>Great minds of the Western tradition</u> [Cassette recording]. Chantilly, VA: The Teaching Company.

Electronic Sources

Although the rules for documenting electronic sources have undergone a number of changes since the advent of the Internet, the fifth edition of the APA <u>Publication Manual</u> establishes clear rules for these references. The guidelines are:

1) Direct readers as closely as possible to the information being cited, that is, to specific documents.

2) Provide addresses that work. **Where complete information is not available, provide as much as you can to help the reader find the work cited.**

> **Note:**
> The URL comes at the end of the citation, in the retrieval statement, preceded by a colon. URLs should be divided only after a slash or before a period.

Although the APA manual arranges electronic sources somewhat differently, this manual will use essentially the same categories and arrangement as in the MLA chapter. This is because the needs of student researchers are often not the same as those of professional psychologists. This arrangement should also reduce confusion for those teachers and students who must be familiar with both MLA and APA style.

Document within an Online Scholarly Project, Aggregated database, or Professional Site

To cite specific documents on a Web site, follow the format appropriate to the work retrieved; add a retrieval statement that gives the date of retrieval and the proper name of the database. An item or accession number is not required. Include the following information: author, date, document title, publication information, retrieval statement with date, and the URL. The URL should link directly to the article, if possible.

Note that the URL provided in the first three examples below is for the specific document being cited. The opening page in each case is the following:

Internet Medieval Sourcebook: http://www.fordham.edu/halsall/sbook.html

Hoovers Online: http://www.hoovers.com

Thomas Legislative Information: http://thomas.loc.gov

Kempe, M. Treatise of contemplation. In The cell of self-knowledge: Seven early English mystical texts. Internet Medieval Sourcebook. (2001, October 30). Ed. P. Halsall. Fordham University Center for Medieval Studies. Retrieved April 3, 2004, from http://www.ccel.org/g/gardner/cell/cell16.htm

Key changes of the week. (2004, April 3). Hoovers Online. Retrieved April 3, 2004, from http://www.hoovers.com/business_information/--pageid_11035--/global-hoov-index.html

Voting Rights Act of 1965. (1965). Thomas Legislative Information on the Internet. (2004, April 3). Library of Congress, Washington, DC. Retrieved April 3, 2004, from http://ourdocuments.gov/doc.php?doc=100

Additional examples from aggregated databases

Fairy tale. Britannica Concise Encyclopedia. (2004). Retrieved May 25, 2004, from Encyclopedia Britannica Premier Service: http://www.britannica.com/ebc/article?eu=389473

Hosenball, M. (2003, August 11). Behind Al Qaeda's new hijacking strategy. Newsweek. Retrieved April 3, 2004, from Gale U.S. History Resource Center database.

Kanutsuna. T., & Smith, P. K. (2002). Pupil insights into bullying, and coping with bullying: A bi-national study in Japan and England. Journal of School Violence, 1, 5-29. Retrieved April 3, 2004, from ERIC database. (ERIC no. EJ665585).

Lore, M. (2003, December 15). Minnesota Court of Appeals rejects claim by affordable housing advocates. Minnesota Lawyer. Retrieved April 4, 2004, from Lexis-Nexis database.

Perils of electronic voting. (2004, February 9). New American. Retrieved April 3, 2004, from ProQuest database.

Plant, E. A., & Sachs-Ericsson, N. (2004, February). Racial and ethnic differences in depression: The roles of social support and meeting basic needs. Journal of Counseling and Clinical Psychology, 72, 41-56. Retrieved April 3, 2002, from PyscARTICLES database.

Tohid, O. (2003, December 15). In Pakistan, 'slavery' persists. <u>Christian Science Monitor</u>. Retrieved April 4, 2004, from SIRS Researcher database.

Online book not within a scholarly project

Freud, S. (1931). <u>The interpretation of dreams</u>. Retrieved April 4, 2004, from E-Server database: http://eserver.org/books/interpretation-of-dreams

James, William. (1902). <u>The varieties of religious experience</u>. New York: Longmans, Green. Retrieved April 4, 2004, from Universal Library: http://www.psywww.com/psyrelig/james/toc.htm

Part of an online book

Darwin, C. R. (1909-14). Natural selection; or the survival of the fittest. <u>The origin of species</u>. New York: P. F. Collier. Retrieved April 4, 2004, from Bartleby database: http: www. bartleby.com/11/4001.html

Freud, Sigmund. (1914). Forgetting the names and order of words. <u>Psychopathology of everyday life</u>. London: T. Fisher Unwin. Classics in the history of psychology. Retrieved April 4, 2004, from http://psychclassics.yorku.ca/Freud/Psycho/chap3.htm

Article in online periodical (newspaper, magazine, or scholarly journal)

Article in scholarly journal

Hershock, P. D. (2003). From vulnerability to virtuosity: Buddhist reflections on responding to terrorism and tragedy. <u>Journal of Buddhist Ethics,10</u>. Retrieved April 4, 2004, from BUBL Link: http://bubl.ac.uk/link

Krstic, I. (2002). Rethinking Serbia: A psychoanalytic reading of modern Serbian history and identity through popular culture. <u>Other Voices: The (e)Journal of Cultural Criticism, 2</u>. Retrieved April 4, 2004, from http://www.othervoices.org/2.2/krstic/index.html

Price, T. (2004, March 19). Reforming big-time college sports. <u>The CQ Researcher Online, 14</u>. Retrieved April 5, 2004, from the CQ Researcher database: http://library.cqpress.com/cqresearcher

Newspaper article

Attention deficit linked to TV viewing. (2004, April 5). <u>Washington Post</u>. Retrieved April 5, 2004, from http://www.washingtonpost.com.

Ravitch, D., & Weingartner, R. (2004, April 5). Public schools minus the public. <u>New York Times</u>. Retrieved April 5, 2004, from http://www.nytimes.com

Rourke, B. Looking for a voice in all the wrong places. (2004, April 5). <u>Christian Science Monitor</u>. Retrieved April 26, 2001, from http://www.csmonitor.com/ 2004/0405/p09s01-coop.html

Magazine article or review

Edelstein, D. (2004, March 22). Forget me not [Review of the book <u>Eternal sunshine of the spotless mind</u>]. <u>Slate</u>. Retrieved April 6, 2004, from http://slate.msn.com/id/2097362

Fallows, J. (2002, November). The fifty-first state? <u>Atlantic Online</u>. Retrieved April 6, 2004, from http://www.theatlantic.com/issues/2002/11/fallows.htm

CD-ROM Programs

CD-ROM programs are one of the formats in which aggregated databases are available. To reference material from these sources, follow the format appropriate to the work retrieved and add a retrieval statement that gives the date of retrieval and the proper name of the database. It is not necessary to state that the information was obtained from a CD-ROM, nor is an item or accession number required.

Clinton, Bill. (1994). [Abstract]. <u>Current Biography Yearbook, 1994</u>. Retrieved April 21, 2004, from Wilson Biographies database.

<u>Dance on disc: The complete catalog of the dance collection of the New York Public Library on CD-ROM</u>. (2003). Boston: Hall. Retrieved April 9, 2004, from Dance on Disc.

Psyche. (1992). <u>Oxford English dictionary</u>. Retrieved April 6, 2004, from Oxford English Dictionary.

Roberts, L. (1999, November 1). Acid rain: Forgotten, not gone. <u>U.S. News and World Report</u> Retrieved April 21, 2004, from SIRS Researcher Mandarin database.

Yatkar-I-Zariran [Memoirs of Zarir]. (2003). In Zoroastrianism. J. B. Hare (Ed.). Retrieved April 6, 2004, from Internet Sacred Text Archive.

Zionism. (1997). <u>Encyclopaedia Judaica</u>. Retrieved April 6, 2004, from Encyclopaedia Judaica.

Other Electronic Sources

In general, to document other electronic sources, follow the recommendations for citing miscellaneous print and nonprint sources, for example, audiovisual media, works of art, etc., modifying the guidelines as appropriate.

Radio or television program

Hoyt, A. (Writer/Director). (1999). Andrew Carnegie: Rags to riches timeline [Transcript]. The richest man in the world: Andrew Carnegie. American Experience. PBSonline/WGBH, Boston. Retrieved April 6, 2004, from http://www.pbs.org/wgbh/amex/carnegie/timeline/f_timeline.html

Gazit, C., & Stewart, D. (Writers/Producers). (2004, April 5). Meltdown at Three Mile Island [Transcript]. American Experience. PBSonline/WGBH. Retrieved April 10, 2004, from http://www.pbs.org/wgbh/amex/three/filmmore/transcript/index.html

The second intifada and the death of Oslo. (2002, October 8). Part 7 of a series The Mideast: A century of conflict [Transcript]. Morning Edition. Retrieved March 24, 2004, from http://www.npr.org/news/specials/mideast/history/transcripts/7th-part.100802.2_nd-intifada.html

Painting, sculpture, or photograph

Lange, D. (1936). Migrant shed worker, northeast Florida [Photograph]. America from the Great Depression to World War II: Black-and-white photographs from the FSA/OWI, 1935-1945. Prints & Photographs Div., Library of Congress. Retrieved from http://memory.loc.gov/ammem/fsowhome.html

Valtman, E. (1961-1991). The cartoonist who came in from the cold [Online presentation]. Swann Foundation. Prints & Photographs Div., Library of Congress. Retrieved April 6, 2004, from http://www.loc.gov/rr/print/swann/valtman/presentation.html

Interview

McGovern, Ray. (2004, March 10). The skeptical spy [Interview with Michael Robbins]. Mother Jones. Retrieved April 6, 2004, from http://www.motherjones.com/news/qa/2004/03/03_400.html

E-mail

E-mail communications from individuals or messages from nonarchived discussion groups or electronic bulletin boards should not be cited in the reference list. Cite them in the text as personal communications.

J. F. Kerry (personal communication, August 17, 2003)

E. M. Kennedy (personal communication, September 4, 2004)

Message posted to a newsgroup

Sutherland, D. (2004, February 22). What happened to Stanley Milgram's subjects? [Msg 4].

Message posted to sci.psychology.research newsgroup at http://groups.google.com/

Message posted to online forum or discussion group

Edmunds, D. (2003, February 6). Examining ADHD/Ritalin [Msg 309.1]. Message posted

to http://www.ivillage.com.

Summary

APA References

To prepare your References page:

- Arrange your source cards in alphabetical order and list your entries in that order.

- Observe APA rules for formatting, capitalization, punctuation, abbreviations, and order within each entry.

- Follow rules for form of each entry, e.g., book, article, database, online publication, etc.

- Make sure that your reference list entries correspond to your in-text citations.

- Double space throughout.

Appendix A
Outlines for Research Papers

Revised Topic Outline for a Research Paper

Thesis Statement:

Topic Sentence for First Major Topic:

Specific Examples, Details

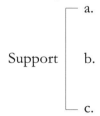

Support
- a.
- b.
- c.

Topic Sentence for Second Major Topic:

Specific Examples, Details

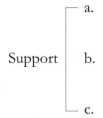

Support
- a.
- b.
- c.

Topic Sentence for Third Major Topic:

Specific Examples, Details

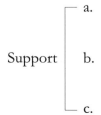

Support
- a.
- b.
- c.

Position Paper Outline

A. Introduction

    1. Issue:

    2. Significance:

    3. Thesis statement:

B. Arguments against your position (Counterarguments)

    1.

    2.

    3.

    4.

C. Arguments in favor of your position

    1.

    2.

    3.

    4.

D. Conclusion

    1. Restatement of thesis statement:

    2. Ideas for going beyond it:

Appendix B
Primary and Secondary Sources

Because researchers sometimes must distinguish between primary and secondary sources, we include here a brief explanation of this distinction. A teacher may require that you use only primary sources for a specific assignment or that you use a certain number of primary sources in addition to secondary ones.

Primary sources are the original words of an individual writer, for example, a speech, an eyewitness report, a personal letter, or remarks in an interview. Examples in specific fields are:

- **Art:** musical compositions, paintings, films, sculptures, artists' sketchbooks, photographs, reproductions, and recordings.

- **Education:** studies, projects, tests and test data, surveys, interviews, observations, statistics, and films.

- **Literature:** novels, short stories, essays, poems, personal letters, autobiographical sketches, diary or journal entries, and memoirs; films, videos, and recordings of readings and performances.

- **Social science:** agency reports, government records, historical documents, eyewitness accounts, interviews, speeches, case studies, results of surveys, presidential tapes, and market research.

- **Science:** results of experiments and tests; reports of observations and discoveries by those conducting the experiments.

Primary source material

- May be an original document such as the Magna Carta, the Declaration of the Rights of Man and Citizen, the Treaty of Ghent, or the U.S. Constitution.

- Often provides direct knowledge of a historical period, for example, the diary of someone who lived during the 1920s.

- Gives information that is first-hand but not necessarily free from bias.

- Is often the subject of a literary research paper. Amy Tan's novel <u>The Joy Luck Club</u> might be your primary source, while reviews, critical articles, and biographical information would be secondary sources.

Secondary sources are works **about** individuals and their work, for example, biographies, histories, critical studies of novels, and discussions of scientific findings. Examples include:

- **Art:** critical and analytical articles, reviews, and biographies.

- **Education:** articles evaluating educational practices, reports, and books about educational issues and problems.

- **Literature:** articles, reviews, analyses, critical studies, and books about literary works and writers.

- **Social science:** articles and books about social issues or historical events; biographies; and newspaper and magazine reports.

- **Science:** review, discussion, and interpretation of scientific experiments, observations, and controversies.

Secondary sources

- Include critical and analytical reviews and discussion of what may be your primary source, for example, a novel, historical document, survey, or scientific experiment.

- May be primary sources in a different study; for example, you may use the <u>Washington Post</u> as a **primary source** for a study of objective reporting in newspapers but as a **secondary source** for a paper describing life on Capitol Hill in the 1960s.

- Require close examination to evaluate objectivity, depth, and timeliness and to distinguish between fact and opinion.

To summarize: Primary sources are **by** the writer who did the work; secondary sources are **about** the person and his or her work. Some research papers use only one kind of source material while others require both. Make sure that you understand the difference <u>before</u> you start looking for sources for your research project.[*]

---

[*] The following books were useful in the preparation of this chapter: James B. Lester and James Lester, Jr., <u>Writing Research Papers: A Complete Guide</u>, 10th ed. (New York: Longman, 2002), and Brenda Spatt, <u>Writing from Sources</u>, 6th ed. (New York: St. Martin's, 2002).

Appendix C
Model Research Papers

The research papers that follow are examples of fine student work. These essays combine creative thinking, careful research, mature writing, and strenuous revision. They exemplify the skills emphasized throughout this manual: narrowing the topic, formulating a forceful thesis statement, finding adequate support from a variety of sources, integrating borrowed material with the author's own ideas, and documenting accurately. In each essay we have double-underlined the thesis statement and have highlighted the method of development and major topic sentences to make it easier for readers to see how these important elements are connected.

The first three essays, on topics in the humanities and in MLA style, are by recent graduates of Walt Whitman High School in Bethesda, Maryland. The fourth essay, by a student at the Maret School in Washington, DC, is on a scientific topic and exemplifies APA style. We are especially grateful to these students' teachers, who not only taught them well but also facilitated the inclusion of their work in this manual. Needless to say, these essays are reprinted with the students' permission.

Cornell 1

Portia Cornell

AP Eng. Lang., Per 6

December 15, 2006

Surviving Adolescence with Magic

The familiar words "Once upon a time" evoke, for many, feelings of nostalgia

and warmth; they strike a chord of remembrance. A traditional fairy tale is more

memorable than many contemporary children's stories because of its capacity to delve

into some of the darker facets of human nature; despite the best efforts of the

Victorians to soften and dilute these tales for the nursery, they have kept their folklore

essence. This honesty makes the fairy tale appealing to children curious about the

realities of the adult world. "Rapunzel," a fairy tale retold by the Grimm brothers,

despite its layers of fantasy, is not afraid to "tell it like it is." It deals with some of the

important aspects of adolescent growth and development: physical self and sexuality,

rebellion, and parent-child relationships. By symbolizing the perils of adolescence,

Rapunzel's story of imprisonment and escape provides a child, particularly a young girl,

with comfort and guidance as she prepares to enter this stormy time of life.

"Rapunzel" offers a young girl confidence about her changing body and emerging

sexuality. Rapunzel's body has tremendous magical power: her tears cure the prince's

blindness, and her long tresses allow him to climb up the tower. This power of

Rapunzel's body to bring her success reassures the child that her own body will contain such strength (Bettelheim 149). As puberty begins to affect a young girl, the changes it

inflicts cause her to feel awkward and unsure. "Rapunzel" helps to curb these

insecurities by telling her that, despite these changes, her body still has the means by

which she can grow and succeed. Young girls must deal not only with the changes in

their outward appearance but also with the emotional effects of adolescence, namely, an

emerging sexuality. Psychologist Mary Pipher explains that to come to terms with this

newfound sexual self, a girl must learn how to make sexual decisions and to be

comfortable with her sexuality, a task that may be one of the major hurdles of young

adulthood (205). Rapunzel's golden hair is a complex symbol. Marina Warner points out

that "maidenhair can symbolize maidenhead, and its loss, too, and the flux of sexual

energy that this releases . . ." (374). This sexuality, in the form of Rapunzel's long tresses,

enables her to form a relationship with the prince; it lets him reach her in the tower.

According to the Grimm version, Rapunzel was "dreadfully frightened when she saw

the prince, for she had never seen a man before" (340). Similarly an adolescent girl

seems to wake up one morning and suddenly "see" the opposite sex as she discovers the

different relationships she might have. The fairy tale reminds the young adolescent that

she is not alone in her surprise. The young teenager learns that, just as Rapunzel's new

sexuality lets her form a loving bond with the prince, these new feelings will let the

teenager form similar bonds. "Rapunzel" does not, however, make its message too

blatant. Bettelheim argues that since the tale does not mention marriage, nor does it

Cornell 3

explicitly describe a sexual relationship between the two lovers, one should understand the bond as symbolic of pure love rather than as raw sexuality (115). Thus the story, while encouraging the formation of new relationships, does not promote promiscuity.

Rapunzel's story also prepares a child for the painful rebellion and process of development that she must undergo to form her individual personality. Pipher describes the difficulties of adolescence as a time when girls "crash and burn in a social and developmental Bermuda Triangle" (19). She adds that without this sometimes painful period of rebellion, a young person, though healthier in the short term, may not develop into a creative, independent adult (92). This stage will be difficult for the child and will be marked by immaturity, struggle, and fear as she tries to make decisions on her own for the first time. But ultimately the struggle shapes her into a more vibrant, thoughtful personality. By following this pattern of struggle and by encouraging autonomy, "Rapunzel" guides young women through this process. Another distinguished folklorist, Maria Tatar, considers Rapunzel's tower the symbolic representation of a mother's protective rules and admonitions. Far from being cautionary elements, as people often interpret them, these warnings become encouragement as they rouse the curiosity and sense of adventure in the young protagonist (166). Rapunzel's imprisonment becomes a metaphor for the strictures a young teenager feels compelled to test, such as her parents' demands for curfews or observance of religious rules, and thus encourages the adolescent to stretch beyond these bonds to become independent.

The tale does not pretend, however, that the transition will be smooth. According to Max Luthi, Rapunzel's story represents a growing process in which the adolescent must first overcome the hardships of loss and danger to achieve lasting happiness (112). Citing a Mediterranean version in which the witch kidnaps Rapunzel after biting off her ear, Luthi sees the tale as one of a scary passage into adolescence. For the modern teenager, this kidnapping might be analogous to a change of schools or a parental trip to Europe that leaves the children seemingly abandoned at home. The young must also face the effects of their immaturity. For example, when the witch discovers the two young lovers, the prince rashly flings himself from the tower window, gouging his eyes out on the thorns below. Bettelheim notes the childishness of the lovers' behavior toward the witch, and their despair and hopelessness after she banishes them. These failures, however, are part of the learning process and the development of a responsible self (Bettelheim 149-50). As adolescents ride an emotional roller coaster, they not surprisingly have a tendency toward melodrama. By exaggerating this quality in the prince and Rapunzel, the tale offers comfort and guidance. It cautions a child to think through her problems and to consider consequences rationally. Because the prince eventually regains his sight, the implication is that one can overcome youthful errors and achieve happiness.

For an adolescent, establishing a separate identity means breaking parental ties, and "Rapunzel" sympathizes with the difficulties of the parent-child relationship. It

Cornell 5

embodies the resentment adolescents often feel toward their parents. Rapunzel's parents are an archetypal "dysfunctional family" as her mother's silly, impractical desire leads to the family's breakdown (Tatar 58). This aspect appeals to a teenager's tendency to suspect that her parents are somehow responsible for her unhappiness. The realization that her parents are not perfect leads the young teenager to feel less close to them, and Rapunzel, after her incarceration in the tower, begins to forget her true mother. As Luthi points out, because Rapunzel forgets her parents does not mean she no longer loves them, just that she needs to become emotionally independent of them (114).

In a shift of emphasis, the tale turns from the teenager's perception of a negligent parent to her view of an overprotective, controlling one. Rapunzel moves from her true parents' home into the tower of the witch, where her imprisonment symbolizes the oppression an adolescent often feels from her parents. With this shift, the tale focuses on the main conflict of adolescence. As Pipher maintains, the teenager must give up the protection of her parents' loving relationship just when she feels most vulnerable because of the changes in her life (23). The witch's selfish and seemingly cruel imprisonment becomes comforting to the child who is not yet ready to give up this protection (Bettelheim 148). So "Rapunzel" deals with a teenager's tumultuous feelings about her parents with an exaggerated characterization of all parents' natural desire to keep their child safe from the world.

This approach keeps the balance between encouraging independence and inciting

Cornell 6

fear and uneasiness. In <u>The Tower and the Well</u>, a study of Madame D'Aulnoy's fairy

tales, Amy DeGraff observes that a tower often represents a place where the inner self

develops. The youth's experience and maturation within the tower suggest that

"resistance to parents' authority is a prerequisite to autonomy" (71). This seems equally

true in "Rapunzel." Rapunzel must struggle within the confines of the witch's tower

until her experience with the prince helps her to break free. The adolescent understands

from the tale's message that only as she "breaks free" from her parents' "bonds" can she

become an autonomous individual. One final aspect of this story makes it an apt

metaphor for parent-child relationships: the fate of the witch. Unlike the stepmother in

"Snow White," who must dance herself to death in her red hot shoes, or the stepmother

in "Cinderella," who must live out her life as a servant, the witch-like foster mother

suffers no act of vengeance. As Rapunzel and the prince have grown out of their

adolescent turmoil, they feel no need to punish. So teenagers can hope to grow into

independent adults without harboring resentment toward their sometimes inadequate

parents.

     "Rapunzel" captures a child's interest with its magic and fantasy and then keeps

that interest by avoiding moralistic lectures and by playing up to a naturally adventurous,

rebellious youth. Because it deals with serious issues of sexuality and rebellion, the tale is

intriguing and memorable not only to a child but also to young people who are

undergoing the transition from adolescence to adulthood. Though a child may not

Cornell 7

recognize the tale's symbolism or relevance immediately, the deeper meaning of

"Rapunzel" may have a profound effect that lasts well beyond the nursery into later

years.

Works Cited

Bettelheim, Bruno. <u>The Uses of Enchantment: The Meaning and Importance of Fairy Tales</u>. New York: Knopf, 1976.

DeGraff, Amy Vanderlyn. <u>The Tower and the Well: A Psychological Interpretation of the Fairy Tales of Madame D'Aulnoy</u>. Birmingham: Summa, 1984.

Luthi, Max. <u>Once Upon a Time: On the Nature of Fairy Tales</u>. Bloomington: U of Indiana P, 1970.

Pipher, Mary. <u>Reviving Ophelia: Saving the Selves of Adolescent Girls</u>. New York: Ballantine, 1994.

"Rapunzel." <u>The Grimms' Fairy Tales</u>. Ed. Jacob Grimm and Wilhelm Grimm. Stamford, CT: Longmeadow, 1987.

Tatar, Maria. <u>The Hard Facts of the Grimms' Fairy Tales</u>. Princeton: Princeton UP, 1987.

Warner, Marina. <u>From the Beast to the Blond: On Fairy Tales and Their Tellers</u>. New York: Farrar, 1994.

Rosensweig 1

Jason Rosensweig

AP Eng. Lang., Per. 3

December 15, 2006

The Holy Grail: More than a Christian Cup

The collection of tales known as the Arthurian legends has remarkable depth, richness, and cultural significance. A blend of Celtic, Welsh, German, and French elements, the saga of Arthur Pendragon provides adventure and romance as well as moral and spiritual ideals. Wandering minstrels spread these stories throughout Europe during the Middle Ages, and a number of written versions eventually appeared, including Sir Thomas Malory's <u>Morte d'Arthur</u>, the major text in English. Among the tales, that of the quest of the Holy Grail remains both popular and puzzling. <u>Although the quest may seem to have significance primarily for Christians, its theme of the search for purity, perfection, and divine inspiration has parallels in Jewish thought as well</u>.

To appreciate the symbolism and meaning of the Quest, one must understand the story's historical background. A heroic king named Arthur reigned during the fifth century CE, and for centuries after his death, a collection of stories about his life and the adventures of his court, known as <u>The Matter of Britain</u>, circulated. The first comprehensive telling of Arthur's exploits appeared in 1135 in Geoffrey of Monmouth's <u>History of the Kings of Britain</u>. Then, in 1200 CE, the French poet Robert de Boron linked the then undeveloped Holy Grail story to Arthur's, and within several decades an

Rosensweig 2

anonymous group of French authors compiled the five-part Vulgate Cycle, the first complete collection of all the elements of the Arthurian tales known today. The fifth section of the Vulgate Cycle was <u>La Queste del Saint Graal</u>. Malory's work, which appeared in 1450, remains the most widely read version (O'Neal 37-47). Malory, however, condensed the Vulgate's account; the older Vulgate version, translated by P.M. Matarasso, which scholars consider the more authoritative, serves as the primary source for this paper.

The Quest for the Holy Grail is more than a search for a famous object; it is a symbolic journey toward spiritual and bodily purity. Roger Loomis describes it as both "a vain following after wandering fires" and "the arduous search for supreme mystical experience" (1), thus suggesting that for many, the quest will end in failure. The angelic hermit who commands the knights onto the Quest expresses its essence in this way:

> None shall take maid or lady with him on this Quest without falling into mortal
> sin; nor shall anyone set out unless he be shriven or seek confession, for no man
> may enter so high a service until he is cleansed of grievous sin and purged of
> every wickedness. For this is no search for earthly things but a seeking out of the
> mysteries and hidden sweets of Our Lord, and the divine secretes through which
> the most High master will . . . show the marvels of the Holy Grail and reveal that
> which the heart of man could not conceive nor tongue relate. (Matarasso 47)

After the quest begins, meandering plot elements of wandering knights coalesce as four knights travel throughout Britain in search of the Grail. Each repeatedly faces trials of his individual commitment to purity and his desire to help others. Galahad's rescue of the Castle of Maidens from the seven evil knights exemplifies the constant interplay of the knights' struggle for perfection and the plight of the commoners. According to Loomis, it signifies "Christ's descent into hell to release the souls of the righteous, and the liberation of the pure souls from the seven deadly sins" (180). This symbolic rescue is similar to Moses' salvation of the Israelites and the Exodus that ensued. In the analogy in the Quest, the perfect knight, Galahad, is compared to Christ; the story relates that scores of other aspiring rescuers have failed in the past. Galahad must not only conserve his purity throughout his travels, but he must also aid others to the best of his ability, just as observant Jews must pursue tikun olam in fulfilling the 613 commandments that fill the Torah and drive their daily lives.

In Hebrew, the fine line between perfection and betterment is evident in the words tikun olam, sometimes translated as the betterment of the world, sometimes as the perfection of the world. As Professor Reuven Kimelman observes, "Tzedaka [charity] may not save us, but it makes us worth saving" (Telushkin 513), so it is an essential part of the moral life. Rabbi Hillel articulates the central role that tikun olam plays in Judaism: "What is hateful unto you do not do unto your neighbor, the rest is commentary" (121). Just as Galahad, the chivralous knight, is charged to save imprisoned maidens and to succor those in need, so devout Jews are counseled to

Rosensweig 4

pursue <u>tikun olam</u>.

In the Quest, divine inspiration and prophecy propel the story. The vision revealed to all the Knights of the Round Table is the inspiration that instigates the journey. Abstract and dreamlike, this vision is at the same time vivid and concrete. For those who experience it, there is a sense of God's immediate presence, and this has a profound effect: "Those persons who suddenly saw the Grail in front of them, open and unconcealed, suffered a severe shock"; some endured memory lapses and vertigo that lasted for days (Goodrich 2). The story intertwines divine prophecies with the events of the narrative. For example, the prediction that the high prince Galahad will come occurs several times: in the inscription on the Siege Perilous, the abbey that houses Galahad's white shield for centuries before his arrival, and by the Maimed King, who awaits his savior for many years. As Loomis notes, "The Grail is a symbol of grace, and grace is God's love for man" (183). The extent to which an individual achieves it depends on his ability to earn it (Matarasso 16). Judaism also teaches of divine providence, the belief that God ordains all events (Telushkin 550). Within this framework, observant Jews, like the knights of the Quest, pursue spiritual and bodily perfection. Both are reaching out for God's love, the inspiration to maintain purity and to do good in the world.

As an allegory of the search for spiritual perfection, the Quest for the Holy Grail is also a study of imperfection and its consequences. Matarasso points out that the story "presents us with different types of humanity at varying degrees of spiritual development" (17). It implies the need to understand impurity and to be lenient toward those who do not achieve perfection. Although only Galahad is wholly successful, obtaining the vision of the grail and ascending to heaven, there are partial rewards for those who strive but fail. The other knights—Bors, Lancelot and Ector—catch only a glimpse. Lancelot's failure is not necessarily a reflection of his errors but of his inability to commit to future purity. Divine agents, usually monks or hermits, give him frequent opportunities to renounce his sordid affair with Guinevere, but he knows he is incapable of denying his lust. If he had confessed and resolved to future perfection, he might have achieved the Grail completely. Such a commitment is like that of a Jew who absolves himself on Yom Kippur and looks to the new year. The teaching of Judaism is clear: "The repentant sinner should strive to do good with the same faculties with which he sinned . . . . With whatever part of the body he sinned, he should now engage in good deeds" (Telushkin 543). Lancelot must extend his righteousness from his knightly side to his personal side by ending his affair with Guinevere; he cannot compensate for his adulterous deficiency with righteousness elsewhere. The commitment to reform as a requirement of the acceptance of sin and imperfection plays a central role both in the Quest and in Judaism.

The Quest illustrates humanity's pursuit of righteousness and spirituality. In the Vulgate's Queste del Saint Graal, Christian monks and scholars added biblical quotations and commentary that give the story a decidedly Christian flavor, despite its non-

Rosensweig 6

Christian origins. The moral foundation, however, and the themes of purity and man's relationship to God reveal the story's parallels to Jewish teaching as well. The knightly heroes, in both their achievements and mistakes, can serve as literary role models for both religions. And the values that the Quest celebrates—spiritual perfection, purity of mind and body, service to others, and betterment of the world—transcend their embodiment in specific religions and speak to all mankind.

Works Cited

Goodrich, Norma Lorre. <u>The Holy Grail</u>. New York: Harper, 1992.

Loomis, Roger Sherman. <u>The Grail: From Celtic Myth to Christian Symbol</u>. Princeton: Princeton UP, 1991.

Matarasso, P. M., trans. <u>The Quest of the Holy Grail</u>. Baltimore: Penguin, 1969.

O'Neal, Michael. <u>Great Mysteries: King Arthur</u>. San Diego: Greenday, 1992.

Telushkin, Rabbi Joseph. <u>Jewish Literacy</u>. New York: Little, 1974.

Simon Chin

AP Eng. Lang., Per. 5

May 10, 2007

Censorship of <u>As I Lay Dying</u>: Yoknapatawpha in Peril

Free expression and discourse have long been pillars of democratic societies.

Without a free flow of opinions in the marketplace of ideas, a democracy based upon

citizen input and activism cannot properly function. However, governments of all forms,

including representative democracies, have engaged in censorship or restriction of various

forms of speech and expression. In 1644, John Milton published <u>Areopagitica</u>, one of the

first major works advocating free speech, in which he vigorously protested the policies of

prior restraint and censorship by the British parliament. Milton argued that diversity of

opinion is essential to the pursuit of knowledge: "Where there is much desire to learn,

there of necessity will be much arguing, much writing, many opinions; for opinion in good

men is but knowledge in the making" (22). Censorship wars continue to rage, and Milton'

ideas are at the heart of contemporary free speech arguments. For modern societies, the

central dilemma of censorship is discerning the distinction between legitimate restriction

and unjustified limitation of speech and expression.

America's policy of local control of education has created a system that allows

individual school districts considerable power to decide which books to include in the

curriculum and which books to restrict or ban. Even the greatest works of literature are

Chin 2

not immune to challenge. Over the past decades, two school districts have banned and

two others have challenged, on religious and social grounds, Nobel Laureate William

Faulkner's 1930 classic As I Lay Dying (Doyle 36). Although objectors may consider the

language or content of the novel offensive, As I Lay Dying should be retained in the

curriculum because it is a valuable work of literature that merits reading and critical

study by high school students.

Religious reasons formed the basis of the bans of As I Lay Dying in two

Kentucky school districts. The objectors to the novel in Graves County and Louisville

both cited passages in which characters used God's name in vain and questioned the

existence of God as grounds for the novel's removal (Attacks 106). The greatest

controversy surrounded a passage in which a character asks, "If there is a God, what the

hell is He for?" (Faulkner 15). The bans received considerable support from Christian

fundamentalists. The Graves County Baptist Association wrote a letter to the local

school board applauding its ban, and one Baptist preacher commented that

bookbanning was the first step in "the march for decency" (Foerstel 38-39). In

Louisville, one parent commented, "I spent years teaching my children that there is a

God and what He is for" (Attacks 106). The objectors, believing that the novel

undermined Christian values, successfully lobbied to have the novel banned in their

respective school districts.

The censorship of books for religious reasons, however, is unconstitutional as it

Chin 3

constitutes official suppression of ideas and violates the Establishment Clause of the First Amendment. Federal courts have repeatedly ruled that school districts cannot ban books to suppress religious, political, or social ideals (Bjorklun 45-46). The Eleventh Circuit Court of Appeals noted in <u>Virgil v. School Board of Columbia County, Fla.</u> (1989) that there are "rather strict limits on school board discretion to use the curriculum to advance religious views in violation of the Establishment Clause" (41-42). Thus, the actions of the school boards in Graves County and Louisville are in clear violation of the First Amendment prohibition of state establishment or endorsement of religion. Supreme Court Justice William Brennan wrote in <u>Keyishian v. Board of Regents</u> (1967) that the First Amendment "does not tolerate laws that cast a pall of orthodoxy over the classroom . . . . The nation's future depends upon leaders trained through wide exposure to that robust exchange of ideas which discovers truth 'out of a multitude of tongues,' [rather] than through any kind of authoritative selection" (Foerstel 69-70). The censorship of <u>As I Lay Dying</u> on religious grounds unduly restricts students' free access to ideas and undermines the aim of providing students with a broad-based education.

Censorship cases involving <u>As I Lay Dying</u> have also centered on the appropriateness of the novel's content for high school students. Along with its religious objections, the Graves County School District banned the novel for containing "offensive and obscene passages referring to abortion" (Doyle 36). In Pulaski County, Kentucky, parents objected to the novel because of a passage about masturbation (36).

Chin 4

Although school districts may not ban books to suppress ideas, the Supreme Court did rule

in <u>Hazelwood v. Kuhlmeier</u> (1988) that schools can ban books for legitimate educational

reasons (Bjorklun 44). The <u>Hazelwood</u> decision warned though that "the educational

suitability of the books . . . must be the true reason for the books' exclusion and not just

pretextual expressions for exclusion because the board disagrees with the religious or

philosophical ideas expressed in the books" (44). Based on this standard, a court would

probably strike down the Graves County ban but uphold restrictions based on reasons

similar to those cited in Pulaski County. Book restrictions based on educational concerns ar

on solid ground in the United States.

Nevertheless, school districts should refrain from banning <u>As I Lay Dying</u> as

Faulkner's inclusion of "mature" themes is an integral element of his stream-of-

consciousness technique and has legitimate artistic justification. <u>As I Lay Dying</u> does not

have a traditional narrative structure but instead consists of 59 short internal monologues

told from various characters' points of view (Volpe 127). Literary critic Edmond Volpe

writes, "In these brilliant short monologues, Faulkner permits his speakers to characterize

themselves. Each thought is shaped by the background and personality of the speaker"

(128). Faulkner wanted the monologues to portray the inner thoughts of his characters,

and his success in delving into the psychology of his characters gives his novel its

brilliance. Professor Olga Vickery of the University of Southern California writes, "The

Bundren family provides a locus for the exploration of the human psyche in all its

complexity without in the least impairing the immediate reality of character and action"
(50). A literary approach based on realism necessitates an author's inclusion of all
relevant details of the lives of his characters.

Federal Judge John Woolsey deemed such a stream-of-consciousness approach as
having artistic merit in his landmark 1933 decision removing the ban on James Joyce's
Ulysses. Woolsey wrote that Joyce's attempt to achieve his objective required him "to
incidentally use certain words which are generally considered dirty . . . and has led at
times to what many think is a too poignant preoccupation with sex" (2). Woolsey
concluded that the profanity and graphic details of Ulysses are not gratuitous but that
"each word of the book contributes like a bit of mosaic to the detail of the picture which
Joyce is seeking to construct for his readers" (2). Such an analysis is applicable to As I
Lay Dying. Although critics may object to certain aspects of the novel, school districts
should value the novel as a work of art that exemplifies a significant twentieth century
literary technique.

Two challenges to As I Lay Dying also cited the novel's profanity and Southern
dialect as justification for the novel's removal from schools. In both incidents, the
school districts in question, Pulaski County in Kentucky and Carroll County in
Maryland, ultimately decided to retain the novel (Doyle 36). The school districts made
the right decision. The language in As I Lay Dying is not gratuitous and is relatively tame
by modern standards. Attorney and author William Noble sums up the novel's possibly

Chin 6

objectionable content: "There are no graphic sex scenes, no strings of four-letter words,

no subtle appeals to the prurient interest. . . . There is the occasional use of the epithet,

. . . the reference to and urging of an abortion, the sprinkling of curse or mild-enough

blasphemies. And that is all" (12). In an age when high school students have frequent

exposure to such language through television, movies and other media outlets, efforts to

ban As I Lay Dying for its mild profanity are naïve and misguided.

However, the greatest danger in the debate over Faulkner's language lies in the

challenges to the novel for its Southern dialect. For centuries, the world's greatest

writers, from Shakespeare and Dickens to Twain and Steinbeck, have employed the

language and dialect of their periods and locales. To suggest that a novel is inappropriate

because of the dialect ascribed to its characters delves into issues that strike at the core

of what makes outstanding literature. Even though parents or school board members

may find the language of As I Lay Dying coarse or uneducated, Faulkner's use of dialect

is an essential part of his literary and artistic technique. Vickery states the case forcefully:

"As a part of his attempt to render the truth of man, Faulkner has assiduously explored

the problem of language, both from the point of view of technique and as an index of

human behavior. The latter involves the examination of verbal patterns that dominate

the South and subtly mold the individual, his society, and his tradition" (266). Readers

should not isolate Faulkner's language from his ideas and themes, as the Southern

dialect is a vital aspect of his novels' richness and profundity. Vickery argues, "Since language is at once the foundation and product of social intercourse, it cannot be separated from the matrix of personal and communal experience" (266). To fully explore the complexities and intricacies of the American South, Faulkner had to employ authentic language and tone.

As I Lay Dying is ultimately important because it provides a window through which to view human nature. The antics of the Bundren family, which are alternately tragic and comic, are representations of the disparate aspects of humanity. Volpe writes, "The complexities and the contradictions of the human personality are exposed and explored, and the ultimate result is the reader's awareness of the amusing and tragic incongruities between the individual's vision of himself and his neighbor's view of him" (128-129). The universal themes that emerge from Faulkner's novel give As I Lay Dying its lasting impact. School districts that ban the novel are denying students the value of Faulkner's profound observations about humanity.

The literary value of As I Lay Dying clearly outweighs any qualms about the novel's language or content. Despite objections and challenges to the novel, school boards should affirm the necessity of a free flow of ideas and refrain from banning a literary masterpiece. Parents or school board members who seek to shelter students from aspects of the novel they deem objectionable are stunting students' intellectual growth and sacrificing knowledge on the altar of misguided piety.

Chin 8

Works Cited

Attacks on the Freedom to Learn: 1994-1995 Report. Washington: People for the
American Way, 1995.

Bjorklun, Eugene C. "School Book Censorship and the First Amendment." Educational
Forum Fall 1990: 37-46.

Doyle, Robert P. Banned Books: 1996 Resource Guide. Chicago: American Library
Association, 1996.

Faulkner, William. As I Lay Dying. New York: Vintage, 1930.

Foerstel, Herbert N. Banned in the U.S.A.: A Reference Guide to Book Censorship in
Schools and Public Libraries. Westport, CT: Greenwood, 1994.

Milton, John. Areopagitica (1644). Ed. Judy Boss. Renascence Editions. U of Oregon.
1997. 29 Sept. 1999 <http://www.uoregon.edu/~rbear/areopagitica.html>.

Noble, William. Bookbanning in America: Who Bans Books?—And Why. Middlebury,
VT: Eriksson, 1990.

Vickery, Olga W. The Novels of William Faulkner: A Critical Interpretation. Baton
Rouge: Louisiana State UP, 1964.

Volpe, Edmond. A Reader's Guide to William Faulkner. New York: Farrar, 1964.

Woolsey, John M. "Opinion A. 110-59." United States District Court, Southern District
of N.Y. 6 Dec. 1933. Work in Progress. 17 Oct. 1999 <2street.com/joyce/etext/
wool.html>.

Dickinson 1

Jeffrey Dickinson

Subtropical Zone Ecology

Maret School

December 1, 2007

The Osprey: An Overview and Sanibel Snapshot

Before the 1960s, the concept of the natural world as an evolved and interdependent web of organisms was ill formed or nonexistent. Perhaps still reflecting the mentality of the North American frontier, people often thought an animal was worthless unless they could eat it or use its hide or feathers. They hardly ever considered the greater consequences to the organism web as a whole of eliminating a "useless" species. The story of the osprey in recent decades in North America demonstrates our ability to correct poor decisions, as a review of the bird's physical characteristics, habitat, mating and feeding behavior, and threatened survival makes clear. Once universally endangered, the osprey is returning to its former numbers in many places, perhaps led by Florida's Sanibel Island.

The osprey is a large bird of prey, distinguished by its contrasting colors. Its body is dark brown on top and bright white below, dominated by dark brown wings and white legs with sharp black talons. Its white head features a dark brown, horizontal stripe from the eye to the back. Also known as the fish hawk, the osprey is the only raptor whose talons can extend backward, a feature that facilitates its capturing fish. On average, the osprey has a body size of between 22 and 25.2 inches with a wingspan that can reach up to five and a half feet. The design of its bill, typically one to two inches in length, enables it to tear into the flesh of fish when it eats. Closely related to the bald eagle, the osprey presents the same aura of power in its body: the two raptors are often confused, although the osprey's white underside differentiates it.

In North America, the osprey primarily inhabits coastal areas from the Aleutian Islands of Alaska to the Florida Keys. The fish hawk will rarely venture inland, since it searches for food predominantly in water depths of three to six feet. In locating its nest, the osprey prefers a site with a full 360-degree panorama that includes its prospective hunting waters. This preference makes the manmade nesting poles of a place like Sanibel Island, Florida, prime real estate for osprey pairs. From the vantage offered by these pedestals, the birds can see the ocean waters that they continually fish; the nesting poles are typically constructed where their tenants enjoy a view unobstructed by cliffs, tree branches, TV antenna bars, or other obstacles. Over time, nesting ospreys have come to recognize that these artificial platforms are actually safer than more natural nest sites, usually in fixed branches of dead trees, because the platforms are protected against egg-hunting raccoons by large sheet metal pieces which prevent animals from ascending, according to Mark Westall (personal interview, July 11, 2003). In terms of natural enemies, no creature targets the osprey specifically: its population is kept in check primarily by raccoons and other animals eating the eggs.

Dickinson 3

Although small mammals and other birds will occasionally enter its diet, the osprey feeds almost exclusively on fish. The hawk's method of fishing is unique. While searching for food, it soars 30 to 100 feet above shallow water. When it spots a fish, the osprey dives swiftly, head- and feet-first, into the water, snaring and gripping its prey with its razor-sharp talons and specially designed foot-pads. Then the osprey beats its wings mightily to raise its fresh catch up out of the water. Once the snared fish clears the surface, the osprey shakes itself off like a wet canine and turns the fish in its talons so that the head and tail of the bird and fish are parallel—and streamlined for flight. As Elphick points out, the hawk then returns to a favorite roost to eat, pinning the fish down with its talons and tearing at its flesh with its well-shaped beak (2001, p. 217), or it returns to the nest to present the captured meal to its partner and chick(s).

Ospreys are usually monogamous: they will remain with the same mate for long periods of time, often their entire life (Elphick, p. 218). The couple establishes itself through a mating dance in which the pair will circle each other and soar, swoop, and dive together. Once its mating dance is complete, the pair constructs its nest together, a rare practice for birds. The fish hawk constructs its substantial nests, which weigh up to 400 pounds, of small tree limbs and large twigs; the interior of the nest is often lined with moss or seaweed (Elphick, p. 219). The osprey's annual migration dominates its reproduction cycle. Typically, ospreys found in summer in Florida will migrate in the fall to parts of South America, including Chile and Argentina. The couple will return to the same nest each spring at the beginning of mating season. As egg-laying time approaches, the couple will copulate, the male mounting the female's back. Once the eggs are fertilized, the male will feed the female until the day she lays. Ehrlich (1998) reports that, over the next 32 to 43 days, the male and female take turns incubating. Once the eggs hatch, the male hunts and returns his catch to the nest, where the female will feed it to the young before they can fly, typically a period of 48 to 59 days. Because their young have a relatively high chance of survival, fish hawks normally produce only one or two chicks per nest each year. Other animals, like loggerhead turtles, which have only a 1-in-10,000 chance of surviving to adulthood, produce 100-200 eggs per clutch to increase chances of a successful hatch.

Much of the attention focused on the osprey and its numbers in recent decades results from the one-time use in the United States of the pesticide dichlorodiphenyltri-chloroethane ($C_{14}H_9Cl_5$), better known as "DDT." "DDT: An introduction" (Duke University, 1996) notes that DDT was first used in World War II to protect soldiers from malaria; after the war, farmers realized that the chemical combination also worked as an extremely effective insecticide for their farms, virtually eliminating common pests. No one realized that DDT had a downside for another decade or so, when, in the late 1950s, researchers studying worms were surprised to discover DDT levels in the worms high enough to kill the robins that consumed them. Furthermore, in the higher trophic levels of the food chain, the accumulation of a pesticide like DDT builds. As the DDT

Dickinson 5

applied to farmers' fields drained into nearby waterways and worked its way through the

food chain as fish gobbled up infected insects, the chemical collected in the tissues of

fish. Then, as birds of prey ate the fish, they suffered further effects: although the DDT

accumulation did not kill them outright, it altered their calcium balance. When they laid

their eggs, the calcium structure of the shell became too thin to support even the weight

of the growing embryo within the shell, according to Ehrlich, Dobkin, and Wheye

(1988). As the thinner shells cracked, fewer and fewer offspring survived. The effect of

DDT on the osprey population was indeed severe, especially considering the paucity of

eggs laid annually. In 1972, after ornithologists established that this problem was

decimating the production of young raptors in the higher food-chain levels, the United

States banned the use of DDT. Within a decade, the population of birds of prey like the

bald eagle and the osprey had rebounded strongly.

On Sanibel Island, Florida, the osprey as an indicator strongly reflects the

nurturing environment established and maintained there. Its mayor, Steve Brown (2003),

points out that Sanibel Island is known as a nature-focused community. Residents

incorporated independently in 1974, splitting decisively from growth-oriented Lee

County in so doing, to battle more effectively the strong pressure from developers and

other pro-growth factions on its strict environmental zoning policies. As a result of this

split, the anti-growth Sanibel Island—once projected by Lee county to support up to

90,000 residents—comfortably supports fewer than 6,000 full-time residents today.

One of Sanibel's leaders in protecting the fish hawk is Mark "Bird" Westall (2003), who provided the following information during an extensive interview. Starting out as a naturalist at the Sanibel-Captiva Conservation Foundation (SCCF) in the late 1970s, Westall noticed that, when an osprey nest was in the way of planned power lines or other improvements on Sanibel, the local power company would simply knock down the offending nest. Westall took an active interest in the osprey and began to monitor bimonthly a comprehensive sampling of 35 nests on the island. Then, in 1981, he launched the International Osprey Foundation (TIOF) to galvanize volunteers to help rebuild the island's osprey population. Today a committed team of TIOF volunteers counts nests all over the island and tracks the number of chicks fledged annually. The volunteers also actively track such information as which banded birds have returned each spring and which nests are active year to year. Furthermore, TIOF publishes plans for constructing nesting platforms and has proven instrumental in guaranteeing their optimal placement on the island. Thanks in large part to the efforts of Westall and TIOF, the platforms today are widely recognized as an essential contributor to the island's recovered and healthy fish hawk population. Westall notes that today, the local power company "bends over backward" to help Sanibel Islanders put up the poles supporting nesting sites.

Throughout North America generally and on Sanibel Island specifically, the evolving story of the osprey is remarkable. The raptor's striking appearance, its fishing

Dickinson 7

technique, its lengthy migration, and its punctual, monogamous return to the same

massive nest each spring fascinate both residents and visitors. However, the osprey was

for decades imperiled from both chemical pollution and extreme loss of habitat, until

both the federal government's ban on using DDT and the proliferation of manmade

platforms began to turn the tide. Thus, the osprey population has resurged generally, in

many places even to pre-WWII levels. And nowhere are conditions more suited to the

osprey's return than Sanibel Island. An affluent and environmentally aware populace

contributing active and committed volunteers, the influence of effective organizations

and individuals offering clear direction, and sound anti-growth and other policies have

combined to make Sanibel Island an ideal spot for the osprey to thrive. Extensive

research has documented the dazzling resurgence of the osprey on Sanibel, making it a

model for interested localities throughout the continent to follow.

References

Brown, S. (2003, June 22). <u>Attitudes toward growth, business, and the environment on Sanibel Island</u>. Unpublished manuscript.

Duke University Chemistry Dept. (1996). DDT: An introduction. In <u>Cruising chemistry: An introduction to the chemistry of the world around you</u>. Retrieved July 10, 2003, from Duke University Web site: www.chem.duke.edu/~jds/cruise_chem/pest/pest1.html

Ehrlich, P. R., ed. (1998). <u>The birder's handbook</u>. New York: Simon and Schuster.

Ehrlich, P. R., Dobkin, D. S., & Wheye, D. (1988). Conservation of raptors. Retrieved July 9, 2003, from Stanford University Alumni Web site: www.stanfordalumni.org/birdsite/text/essays/Conservation_of_Raptors.html

Ehrlich, P. R., Dobkin, D. S., & Wheye, D. (1988). DDT and birds. Retrieved July 12, 2003, from Stanford University Alumni Web site: www.stanfordalumni.org/birdsite/text/essays/DDT_and_Birds.html

Elphick, C. (2001). <u>The Sibley guide to bird life and behavior</u>. New York: Alfred A. Knopf.

Appendix D
Using the Internet

Searching the Internet has become an increasingly important part of students' research projects. It can help you discover valuable information, but it can also gobble up huge amounts of your time. This appendix contains information to facilitate your Internet search. It deals briefly with the following topics: search engines, meta-search tools, subject directories, useful sites, and evaluation of Internet sources. Because engines and sites are subject to rapid change, you should update this section of your manual as you use it, replacing defunct URLs with current ones, eliminating search engines that no longer fire up, and crossing out sites that no longer exist.

Since different search engines have different capabilities, it's probably a mistake to lock onto just one search engine, no matter how much you enjoy using it, and to ignore all the rest. The same is true of meta-search tools, where, on a specific query, you can see one engine finding 30 hits while another registers zero.

Subject directories are often the best place to start your search because in many cases human beings, rather than robots, spiders, and crawlers, have evaluated and categorized the sources. This can save you time and can increase the likelihood that the material you find is reliable and authoritative. In general, you can use the same search options, whether you are using a search engine, meta-search tool, or subject directory. As noted below, a number of search engines are now combined with subject directories. This means you can search both the directory and the Web from a single site.

Search Tool Terminology.

The following terminology about options applies not only to search engines but also to meta-search tools and subject directories.

- Use of + (plus) and - (minus) means to include or exclude. For example, **marijuana -medicinal use** gets you articles about marijuana but omits those devoted to its therapeutic use. Use a space before the sign but not between the sign and the word that follows, e.g., **hate crimes +gays** or **hate crimes –race**, to focus your search. Note that using + and – gets the same result as using the Boolean operators AND and NOT, as explained below.

- Quotation marks mean that a phrase or concept will be treated as a unit; for example, **"black power"** will get you hits about the movement, not every document that mentions "black" or "power" separately. **"Black power" + Stokely Carmichael** will narrow your search further. The search engine will look for an exact match for the phrase in quotation marks.

- Case sensitive refers to the use of capital or lower case letters. It's usually best to use only lower case letters when you search, for example, **"pullman strike,"** or **"mount rushmore."** The search tool will look for the key words, regardless of capitalization.

- To truncate* means to include other forms of your keyword, for example, **Jamaican music*** will find Jamaican **musicians** and **musical** events, not just music. This function is also called <u>using a wild card</u> or <u>stemming</u>.

- Many searches allow the use of Boolean operators, that is, the connectors AND, OR, and NOT to narrow a search. Using AND will return hits with both the terms; OR, with any of the terms; NOT will exclude a term. For example, **ice hockey** gets around 4 million hits. You can narrow the search with **ice hockey AND injuries**, **ice hockey AND injuries AND women**, or **ice hockey AND injuries NOT children**. Some search engines also allow the use of parentheses to avoid confusion in a complicated query. For example, try **opium production AND (Afghanistan OR Pakistan)**, when you want only results about opium production but are interested in operations in either country.

- Some search tools allow the use of the proximity operator NEAR. This means the search will return results for a term if it is close to another. For instance, a search using the query **Microsoft AND (browser NEAR crash)** will get you results where **browser** is within a specified number of words from **crash**. But don't be surprised if your search finds you a few plane crashes as well.

- You can also limit your search by language, domain, file type, date, URL, and a number of other specifications

Search Engines

Search engines are software designed to look through an indexed database of Net documents. They are the key to finding precisely the information that you want from the millions and millions of documents out there in cyberspace. All search engines offer help on their main page; most provide both basic and advanced searches. Although all have the same objective—finding relevant information—they differ in several ways. Below is a brief review of a few of the most popular engines, listed alphabetically. You can find a comparison and analysis of search engines at http://www.searchenginewatch.com and at http://www.notess.com.

AllTheWeb

http://www.alltheweb.com

AllTheWeb has a huge database, is speedy, and includes customization features. Its pre-analysis tool helps teach you how to improve your search technique; there is also a box with useful suggestions. It allows a search of all news categories, or of one specific news resource; its multimedia search capacity is especially strong. It delivers clustered results that link to news stories on your chosen topic. It corrects your spelling if you enter your keywords incorrectly. Use + to include, - to exclude. Not case sensitive; no truncation.

AltaVista

http://www.altavista.com

AltaVista is a popular, comprehensive search engine with a huge index. It consistently and speedily finds useful information, and it searches not only the Web but also news stories, discussion groups, products, images, and video and audio clips. It is especially strong in finding foreign sites and information in foreign languages. You can do a basic or advanced search, or a search for images; you can search by date and by specific domain, e.g., you can add domain:ru to your search term to search only Russian sites. Use quotation marks for exact phrases; use + to require, - to exclude. AltaVista is case sensitive in its basic search but not in its advanced; in both, use * to truncate. In a basic search, use AND, OR, AND NOT, and NEAR to refine.

Google

http://www.google.com

Many experts consider Google both the biggest and the best of the search engines; it provides access to over 4 billion Web pages. It combines features of subject directories and search engines. It finds relevant, prominent Web sites devoted to the issue you're researching. Hit "I'm feeling lucky" to go straight to the first hit on the list, often a home page. In a basic search, inclusion is understood. Use - to exclude; use quotation marks for phrase searching. Not case sensitive; uses truncation automatically to find word variations. You can use Boolean operators in both basic and advanced searches. To search by topic, go to http://directory.google.com; to search U.S. government sites only, go to http://www.google.com/unclesam. For images, go to http://images. google.com; for groups, go to http://www.google.com.

HotBot

http://www.hotbot.com

HotBot provides access to four major search engines: AllThe Web, Google, Teoma, and Yahoo. It's fast, easy to use, and up to date. Its advanced search capability is especially strong. You can search by language, domain, region, specific words, time period, and type of page content, e.g., images, graphics, and multimedia. HotBot provides site clustering and a top ten list of the most popular sites on a given subject. Use + to include, - to exclude; use quotation marks for exact phrase searching. You can also use AND, OR, and NOT. Case sensitive; truncate with *.

Lycos

http://www.lycos.com

Lycos has a large database and features quick, efficient searches. It offers a search engine, several subject directories, and a number of other services. AllTheWeb powers its database and produces useful results; you can also search using Hotbot. The advanced search options include a drop-down menu that allows you to customize your search. You can search specifically for images, sound, video-files, or multimedia. Use + to require, - to remove; use quotation marks for phrase searching. Not case sensitive; no truncation. You can also go to http://dir.lycos.com/Reference/ Searchable%5FDatabases/ where you will find a wealth of information that most search engines fail to uncover.

MSN Search

http://search.msn.com

MSN Search combines a human-powered directory with search engine coverage, using Inktomi and LookSmart. Its basic search results fall into categories such as popular and relevant topics, featured sites, sponsored sites, and Web pages. Use + to include, - to exclude; use quotation marks for phrase searching. Case sensitive; truncation in advanced but not in basic search.

Teoma

http://www.teoma.com

Although Teoma's database is relatively small, it has some useful features. It gathers search results into topic groups, making it easier to narrow your search. Teoma directs you to expert links or major sites for authoritative sources of information relating to your subject. It offers suggestions to help narrow your search. Use quotation marks or dashes without spaces between words for phrase searching, that is, "Bunker Hill Monument" or Bunker-Hill-Monument. Use + to require, - to exclude. Not case sensitive; no truncation.

Wisenut

http://www.wisenut.com

Wisenut has a large database, and it offers speed, relevancy, and flexibility. Like Google, it provides results based on popularity. It organizes results into categories and presents them at the top of the results list. Its Wiseguides are similar to the customized folders that Northern Light made popular. Another special feature is called "Sneak-a-Peek." It allows you to preview another page without leaving Wisenut's results page. Use + to include, - to exclude, and quotation marks for phrase searching. Not case sensitive; no truncation.

Yahoo!

http://www.yahoo.com

Yahoo! now combines a subject directory with a powerful search engine. It is especially useful for general information. There are two ways to search. First, you can use the categories in the directory, which is hierarchical, that is, it goes from general to specific. You might proceed like this: Science→Animals→Worms→Annelids→Leeches, where you can narrow your search further. Yahoo's 14 chief categories are: arts and humanities, business and economy, computers and internet, education, entertainment, government, health, news and media, recreation and sports, reference, regional, science, social science, and society and culture. There are many subcategories and sub-subcategories. Second, you can search the entire collection of Web sites by keyword. Use + to require, - to remove; use quotation marks for phrase searching. Not case sensitive; use * to truncate.

Meta-Search Tools

A meta-search tool allows you to submit your query to several search engines at the same time and then combines the results onto one page. Though slower than search engines like Google or AltaVista, meta-search engines may turn up obscure sources that other engines miss. They allow you to preview what a broad search will involve. Meta-search tools work in much the same way as other search engines: punch in the keyword or phrase, set time parameters, use quotation marks and parentheses, + and -, or Boolean operators AND, OR, NOT, and NEAR. A caution: meta-search engines often provide many results that are paid placement or paid inclusion, and these results are not always clearly identified as such. Although there are a number of meta-search engines, we will describe only five of the most popular ones.

Dogpile

http://www.dogpile.com

Winner of the Best Meta-Search Engine award for 2003, Dogpile is a speedy and powerful engine that combines the efforts of 18 different search engines to search the Web, Usenet, and FTP files. It searches four engines at a time and displays the results; it then goes on to the next four. For a custom search you can select the five engines you prefer. Advanced search and tutorials are available. Results are organized into focused categories, and you can have results displayed either by relevance or by search engine. Dogpile does not eliminate duplicates.

Ixquick

http://ixquick.com

Ixquick is a fast, smart, comprehensive meta-search tool that allows you to select which of its 14 search engines to use. It provides results that individual search engines ranked in the "top ten," and it handles both basic and advanced searches. Ixquick also eliminates duplicates. You can search using natural language or Boolean operators.

Mamma

http://www.mamma.com

Mamma, one of the older meta-search engines on the Web, considers itself the "mother of all search engines." It does a parallel search using several popular search engines, directories, and specialty search sites; it arranges the results based on relevance or sources. Its list of results is relevant and comprehensive.

Metacrawler

http://www.metacrawler.com

Metacrawler links 13 search engines, including Google and AltaVista. You can search using them all for a power search, or you can select the ones you want for a custom search. Metacrawler gives you the results as a uniform list, eliminates redundancy, and ranks the rest according to relevance. It is extremely comprehensive, dependable, and easy to use.

Profusion

http://profusion.com

Profusion offers a combination of nine search engines and directories. You can select all nine or use any combination. Profusion incorporates InvisibleWeb, a search engine that finds contents not indexed by traditional search engines, for example, databases, archived material, and interactive tools. Profusion has a directory of searchable databases that range from highly specialized to general interest, including news and magazine archives, product reviews, government databases, and many more. It sorts results by relevance, search engine, or date, and it provides a useful search analysis page.

Subject Directories

Subject directories are a good place to start your search because they organize Web sites into categories and subcategories which include information that librarians and other experts consider important and useful. The databases of most subject directories are smaller than those of many search engines, so many directories add search engines for supplementary power. A number of subject directories and search engines have merged, and we have already discussed two of the most popular ones, Yahoo! and Lycos. Here are six more that may prove useful in your research.

Britannica.com

http://www.britannica.com

> Britannica does more than provide free access to the encyclopedia, dictionary, and thesaurus; its Internet Guide also finds hundreds of carefully chosen Web sites on a given topic. It has reviewed and rated over 250,000 Web sites and provides a Best Sites column on the search results page. Britannica is strong on academic rather than popular topics. Its archive includes recent and relevant articles from over 70 magazines. The simple search uses keywords or natural language queries; not case sensitive; truncation. To refine your search, use quotation marks for phrase searching, or use Boolean operators and parentheses.

Infomine

http://infomine.ucr.edu

> Infomine was developed and supported by the library of the University of California at Riverside. It provides a scholarly collection of directories on the Web. You can do a direct search using keywords, or you can search the collections by academic discipline. There are additional categories such as cultural diversity, Ejournals, government information, and maps. There are over 9,500 links to Web sites and databases, making Infomine one of the best of the academic-focused subject directories. Use basic or advanced search; not case sensitive; truncation. You can use quotation marks, Boolean operators, and near with numbers from 1 to 20 to indicate range. The advanced search allows additional limitations.

Internet Scout Project

http://scout.cs.wisc.edu

> This site provides Web-based information for educators, librarians, and researchers. It discovers new sites and seeks out the best, providing an annotated report on hundreds of valuable online sources. Despite the project's serious purpose, a visit to this site may provide such pleasures as a tour of the latest exhibition at the Museum of Bad Art, or a multimedia presentation on robots from the Science Museum of Minnesota. Also available are archives of scout-approved sites, including over 16,969 resources, collected over the past nine years. Use keywords in the basic search; in advanced, use quotation marks, - to exclude, and additional limitations.

Librarians Index to the Internet

http://lii.org

> This directory provides carefully selected information about Internet sources. Its index has 14 subject headings, ranging from Arts, Crafts, & Humanities to Sports, Recreation, & Entertainment. In a typical search you might go to Government & Law, to International Governments, and then to Human Rights. There you find, among other resources, a report on prison camps in North Korea. The directory is constantly updated and provides only material that has been reviewed and evaluated for substance and reliability, making it one of the top choices among academically-oriented directories. Both basic and advanced searching is available; in the latter you can limit by fields.

LookSmart

http://www.looksmart.com

> LookSmart is a multipurpose site that combines portal, search engine, and subject directory. One of its unusual features is the live help that is available in case your search ends in failure and frustration. But that shouldn't happen: there is a clearly organized directory to help you navigate through an amazing collection: 250,000 categories and subcategories; 3.5 million articles from over 700 publications. The Web search covers 1.2 billion Web pages. You should beware, however, of material that is paid inclusion or paid placement. For a basic search of the Web, use quotation marks and + or -. In the advanced search, search for all the words you enter or the exact phrase; you can also exclude certain words. In both you can limit your search to magazines or to a specific category.

Open Directory Project

http://www.dmoz.org

> Open Directory is the largest human-edited directory on the Web. It models itself on the Oxford English Dictionary, depending on some 35,000 volunteer editors with expertise in specific areas. Open provides the directory for Netscape, AOL, Google, Lycos, and HotBot, further evidence of the multiple marriages that have taken place among search engines and subject directories. The directory has 16 categories, from Arts to Sports. A simple search uses keywords or Boolean operators, + and -, and truncation. In an advanced search, you can search both categories and sites, and you can limit by field.

Starting Points: Some Useful Sites

There are now thousands of useful sites on the Internet, depending on what you're looking for. For example, to find a recipe for lemon curd, you can go to www.recipes.com. For a directory of Polish sites, try http://www.wp.pl. If you want to find 20,000 links to issues related to women, then http://www.wwwomen.com is your best bet. Here we will list only a handful of sites that have proved especially useful to student researchers. As you search for information, you are likely to turn up many more.

News and Current Events

The three newspapers below all have a fee-based archive for older articles and a free retrieval service for recent ones. All provide reliable, carefully researched material as well as some special features for online users. Many other newspapers are available online, but most experts consider these to be the best.

Los Angeles Times
http://www.latimes.com

> Only same day articles are free.

New York Times
http://www.nytimes.com

> Site registration is required but is free.

Washington Post.
http://www.washingtonpost.com

> The full newspaper for the previous two weeks is free.

 Another excellent source of news is radio and television. All the major networks have Web sites, and they are especially good for late-breaking news. Two noteworthy sites are described below.

CNN Interactive
http://www.cnn.com

> There is no charge for searching the news database for the past month.

National Public Radio
http://www.npr.org

> Good for in-depth coverage of important issues and events.

Three more sites for news are the following:

NewsIndex
http://www.newsindex.com

NewsLink
http://newslink.org

NewsTrawler
http://www.newstrawler.com

Libraries

The Internet Public Library

http://www.ipl.org

You can search for information under the following categories: Arts & Humanities; Associations; Business & Economics; Computers & Internet; Education; Entertainment & Leisure; Health & Medical Sciences; Law, Government & Political Science; Science & Technology; and Social Sciences. The Reference Center includes many full-text books, including almanacs, dictionaries, encyclopedias, atlases, and other reference works. The Reading Room is a gateway to hundreds of online books, magazines, and newspapers.

Library of Congress

http://www.loc.gov

A national collection of books, country studies, historical documents and photographs, databases, catalogs, and Internet links. Under Collections & Services you can search the online catalog for over 12 million items: books, serials, files, manuscripts, maps, and audio and visual materials. THOMAS gets you information about the U.S. Congress (see THOMAS entry below). Access to International Resources is http://international.loc.gov.

National Library of Medicine

http://www.nlm.nih.gov

The National Library of Medicine is the world's largest medical library. It provides information in the following categories: health information, library services, research projects, and current news. You can go to Medline, the biomedical database of the NLM, where PubMed provides access to over 14 million citations from Medline and additional life science journals. There are links to many other resources.

WWW Virtual Library

http://www.vlib.org

Look for information under 14 categories: Agriculture, Business & Economics, Computing, Communications and Media, Education, Engineering, Humanities, Information and Libraries, International Affairs, Law, Recreation, Regional Studies, Science, and Society. There are links to many full-text books and articles from a variety of sources

Information Sources for Specific Disciplines

Literature, Arts, and Humanities

Bartleby: Great Books Online

http://www.bartleby.com

Bartleby's list of online publications includes literature, both fiction and nonfiction, reference, and poetry, all available without charge. Reference books include <u>The Columbia Encyclopedia</u>, <u>American Heritage Dictionary</u>, <u>Bartlett's Famous Quotations</u>, <u>Roget's II: The New Thesaurus</u>, <u>Cambridge History of English and American Literature</u> (18 vols), and Gray's <u>Anatomy</u>. Under Verse you can find, for example, the full-text version of T. S. Eliot's "The Waste Land"; under Fiction, you can find Robert Louis Stevenson's "The Strange Case of Dr. Jekyll and Mr. Hyde."

Cleveland Press Shakespeare Photographs 1870-1982

http://www.ulib.csuohio.edu/shakespeare

Remarkable production photographs of Shakespeare's plays, including stage, film, TV, opera, and ballet versions.

MIT's Complete Works of William Shakespeare

http://www-tech.mit.edu/shakespeare/works.html

Provides the entire text of all of Shakespeare's works.

Mr. William Shakespeare and the Internet

http://shakespeare.palomar.edu

An annotated guide to scholarly Shakespeare resources on the Internet. This site also lists many links to texts, criticism, study guides, and the like.

Here are a few additional sites that provide links and access to thousands of full-text books, poems, plays, essays, and a variety of other publications.

Books on the Internet

http://www.lib.utexas.edu/books/etext.html

Electronic Text Center at the University of Virginia

http://etext.lib.virginia.edu

The EServer

http://eserver.org

Online Books Page

http://digital.library.upenn.edu/books

Project Gutenberg

http://www.gutenberg.net

Universal Library

http://www.ul.cs.cmu.edu

Science

NASA

http://www.nasa.gov

> Source of the latest news and information about NASA science, technology, and strategic enterprises, covering life on earth, humans in space, and exploring the universe. You can browse through popular topics like aeronautics and the space shuttle; you can view videos and listen to audio articles. There are special resources for students and educators.

National Institutes of Health

http://health.nih.gov

> Provides information about clinical trials, drugs, special programs, and a vast array of specific illnesses and health problems. Connects you to Medline, Healthfinder, and many other resources.

Nature

http://www.nature.com/nature

> Offers free online articles on a range of scientific topics in publications from the Nature Publishing Group.

Social Science

Branches of the U.S. Government

You can go directly to a particular branch of government by tapping into the following sites:

White House

http://www.whitehouse.gov

Senate

http://www.senate.gov

House of Representatives

http://www.house.gov

FirstGov

http://www.firstgov.gov

> This site provides one-step access to online U.S. Federal Government resources. It offers information under various categories, including consumer, defense, education, environment, health, public safety, science and technology, and voting and elections. There is information about state and local government, and even the latest word on the most popular baby names (would you believe Emily and Jacob?).

University of Michigan Documents Center

http://www.lib.umich.edu/govdocs

> A well organized site for information about the U.S. government.

Governments on the WWW

http://www.gksoft.com/govt/en/

> Provides links to more than 200 countries and territories.

Hoovers Online

http://www.hoovers.com

> Although Hoovers is a subscription service for information about business and finance, it gives out quite a bit of free information. Its database includes over 12 million companies, and it has reports on companies, research companies, and industries worldwide. It also offers business and market news.

THOMAS

http://thomas.loc.gov

> THOMAS is a major source of legislative information, including current bills, the Congressional Record, and committee action. In addition, it provides reports, directories, links to other branches of government, and historical documents.

U.S. Census Bureau

http://www.census.gov

> Provides population estimates, information about people, business, and geography, including an excellent collection of maps. You can find a detailed portrait of the U.S. economy, and for any state, data and statistics about housing, educational level, employment, poverty, and the like. You can access American FactFinder for additional facts and figures.

Evaluating Web Sites

Because the information you find on the Internet may come from anyone, from last year's Nobel Laureate in Physics to elementary school children to someone confined in an institution for the criminally insane, it is wise to check the reliability of your sources. Whether or not you are required to formally evaluate the sites you visit, the Web Site Evaluation Form on the next page will help remind you of important aspects of sites that you should always check. Teachers will often require students to complete evaluation forms for the Web sites used in their research papers. The evaluation form on pages 231–232 is a modification of one that Marjorie Geldon and Linda Crump created for the Montgomery County (MD) Public Schools. The authors graciously gave their permission to reproduce it here.

Web Site Evaluation Form

Student Name _____Teacher Name _____

1. What is the URL (Uniform Resource Locator), that is, the address of the Web site, found at the top of the Netscape or Internet Explorer screen? The URL normally has the following structure: protocol://domain name/directory/specific file.

http:// _____

2. What is the top-level domain, that is, the name that identifies the sponsor of the site? The domain suffix tells you something about the producer of the site: a company (.com), university or museum (.edu), government (.gov), military (.mil), network (.net), non-profit organization (.org), or country, for example, Canada (.ca), or Latvia (.lv).

.com_____ .edu _____ .gov_____ .mil _____.net_____.org _____ other ____ (.biz, .tv, .info)

3. What is the complete title of the Web site? For example, the name of the site at http://nationalacademies.org/headlines is <u>Science in the Headlines</u>; the site at http://femina.cybergrrl.com, which focuses on women's issues, is called <u>Femina Web Search for Women.</u> A tilde (~) in the address usually indicates a personal home page.

Title of the Web site: _____

4. What is the authority for this site, that is, who is the author, editor, organization, or institution that manages the site? This is often a clue to the trustworthiness of the information. What are the author's credentials?

Authority for this site: _____

On the appropriate line, write the name of the institution with which the author, editor, or institution is associated.

k12 school _____university _____

govt. agency _____organization _____

company _____other _____

Can you contact this site?   yes _____ no _____

How? _____

5. What is the content of the site? Primary sources include original documents, statistics, journals, letters, and images. **Secondary sources** include analysis, criticism, commentary, interpretation, and opinion. Appendix B explains the difference between primary and secondary sources in more detail.

Does this site provide text only? Yes ___ No _____

Does it provide text with graphics? Yes_____ No _____ Multimedia? Yes_____ No _____

Do the graphics and/or multimedia contribute to the topic?   Yes _____ No _____

Does the site include advertising?. Yes _____No ___ Is it distracting? Yes _____No____

Is the material at this site primary/original? _____

Secondary/derived? _____ Both? _____

6. What is the primary purpose of the site?

Inform _____ Persuade _____ Provide facts _____ Offer opinions_____

Does the site have a clear political or philosophical agenda? Yes_____No _____

If yes, what is the site's ideological slant, e.g., right wing Republican, anarchist, socialist, feminist, etc.?

Political agenda: _____

Would you describe the presentation of information as mainly

Subjective, opinionated? _____ Or Objective, unbiased? _____

Both? Explain. _____

7. How current is the site? The latest revision date may be either at the bottom of each page or on the home page only. Many Web sites provide links to other sites. Some may be useful; others may be inactive or irrelevant.

When was this page written or last updated? _____

Are the links active? _____Are they useful? _____

8. How would you rate this Web page? Add your own comments.

Use with caution _____ Good basic information _____

Excellent for this assignment _____

8. Add your own comments:

Appendix E
Citations at a Glance

MLA—Print Resources

Books	Example
One Author Author's Last Name, First Name. <u>Title</u>. Place of publication: Publisher, date.	Martin, Peter. <u>A Life of James Boswell</u>. New Haven: Yale UP, 1999.
Two Authors Author's Last Name, First Name, and 2nd Author's First Name and Last Name. <u>Title</u>. Place of publication: Publisher, date.	Spangenburg, Ray, and Diane K. Moser. <u>The History of Science from the Ancient Greeks to the Scientific Revolution</u>. New York: Facts on File, 1993.
More than three authors First author's Last Name, First Name, et al. <u>Title</u>. Place of publication: Publisher, date.	Jolly, Richard, et al. <u>UN Contributions to Development Thinking and Practice</u>. Bloomington: Indiana UP, 2004.
Editor (ed.) Editor's Last Name, First Name, ed. <u>Title</u>. Place of publication: Publisher, date.	Lim, Shirley, ed. <u>Asian-American Literature: An Anthology</u>. New York: McGraw, 2000.

Periodicals	Example
With an Author Author's Last Name, First Name. "Article Title." <u>Periodical Title</u> Date (day month year) of periodical: page range.	Hersh, Seymour M. "Torture at Abu Ghraib." <u>New Yorker</u> 10 May 2004: 42-47.
Without an Author "Article Title." <u>Periodical Title</u>. Date of periodical (day month year): page range.	"Vietnamese Americans: Lessons in American History." <u>Teaching Tolerance</u> Spring 2004: 31-35.

Print Encyclopedias, Reference Books	Example
With an Author Author's Last Name, First Name. "Article Title." <u>Encyclopedia Title</u>. Edition. date.	Art, Robert J. "United Nations." <u>World Book</u>. 2001 ed.
Without an Author "Article Title." <u>Encyclopedia Title</u>. Place of publication: Publisher. Edition. date.	"Archimedes." <u>Encyclopedia of World Biography</u>. Detroit: Gale. 1998 ed.

MLA—Online Resources

Online Periodicals	Example
Article in Online Newspaper or Newswire Author's Last Name, First Name. "Article Title." <u>Newspaper online site</u> Date (day month year). Access date <URL>. [If no author, begin with article title].	Pierre, Robert E. "In Ohio, Supreme Court Considers Right to Procreate." <u>Washington Post</u> 11 May 2004. 11 May 2004 <http://www.washingtonpost.com/ wp.dynarticles/A15742-2000May10.html>.
Article in Online Magazine Author's Last Name, First Name. "Article Title." <u>Magazine online site</u> Date (day month year). Access date <URL>. [If no author, begin with article title].	Boutin, Paul. "The Case for Staying Off Mars." <u>Wired Magazine</u> March 2004. 11 May 2004 <http://www.wired.com/wired/archive/12.03/ start.html?pg=14>.

Internet Sites	Example
With an Author Author's Last Name, First Name. "Article Title." Date. <u>Title of Internet site or Web page</u>. Editor's Name (if given). Sponsor's Name (if given). Date or latest update (day month year). Access date <URL>.	Gray, Terry A. "A Shakespeare Timeline." 1998. <u>Mr. William Shakespeare and the Internet</u>. Ed. Terry A. Gray. 28 Oct. 2003. 6 May 2004 <http:// shakespeare.palomar.edu/timeline/timeline.htm>.
Without an Author "Article Title." Date. <u>Title of Internet site or Web page</u>. Editor's Name (if given). Sponsor's Name (if given). Date or latest update (day month year). Access date <URL>.	"Black Death, 1348." 2001. <u>Eye Witness to History</u>. Ibis Communications. 2 May 2004. 6 May 2004 <http:// www.eyewitnesstohistory.com/plague.htm>.

Online Encyclopedias, Reference Works	Example
With an Author Author's Last Name, First Name. "Article Title." <u>Encyclopedia Title</u>. Date. Sponsor. Access date (day month year) <URL>.	Katz, Esther. "Margaret Sanger." <u>American National Biography Online</u>. 2000. Oxford UP. 6 May 2004 <http://www.anb.org/articles.home.html>.
Without an Author "Article Title." <u>Encyclopedia Title</u>. Date. Sponsor. Access date (day month year) <URL>.	"Landscape Architecture." <u>Encyclopedia Britannica</u>. 2004. Encyclopedia Britannica Premium Service. 6 May 2004 <http://www.britannica.com/eb/article?eu=48157>.

Subscription Service Databases	Example
Online Database Author's Last Name, First Name. "Article Title." <u>Periodical Title</u> Date (day month year): page range. <u>Name of Database</u>. Name of Service. Name of Library, Location. Access date <URL>.	Herzog, Stephen J. "Wind Energy: Power and Policy." <u>Appraisal Journal</u> Jan. 1999: 24+. <u>Expanded Academic ASAP</u>. InfoTrac. Brattleboro Union High School Lib., Brattleboro, VT. 7 May 2004 <http:// web2.infotrac.galegroup.com>.
CD-ROM Author's Last Name, First Name. "Article Title." <u>Periodical Title</u> Date: page range. <u>Name of Database</u>. Medium. Vendor, Date.	Dunn, Seth. "King Coal's Weakening Grip on Power." <u>World Watch</u> Sept/Oct. 1999: 10-19. <u>SIRS Researcher</u>. CD-ROM. UMI-ProQuest, 2001.

Non-Subscription Databases	Example
With an Author Author's Last Name, First Name. "Article Title." <u>Name of Site</u>. Date. Institution or Organization Name. Access date (day month year) <URL>.	Ebadi, Shirin. "Human Rights and Economic Development." <u>The World Bank Group</u>. 3 May 2004. World Bank. 9 May 2004 <http://worldbank.org >. Path: Archived Features; World Press Freedom Day; Shirin Ebadi Lecture.
Without an Author "Article Title." <u>Name of Site</u>. Date. Institution or Organization Name. Access date (day month year) <URL>.	"List of Member States." <u>United Nations</u>. 24 April 2003. United Nations. 9 May 2004 <http://www.un.org/ Overview/unmember.html>.

APA—Print Resources

Books	Example
One Author Author's Last Name, First & Second Initial. (Date). <u>Title</u>. Place of publication: Publisher.	Martin, P. (1999). <u>A life of James Boswell</u>. New Haven, CT: Yale University Press.
Two—Six Authors Author's Last Name, First & Second Initial, & 2nd Author's Last Name, First & Second Initial. (Date). <u>Title</u>. Place of publication: Publisher. [Give names, initials of up to six authors].	Spangenburg, R., & Moser, D. K. (1993). <u>The history of science from the ancient Greeks to the scientific revolution</u>. New York: Facts on File.
Editor (ed.) Editor's Last Name, First & Second Initial. (Ed.). (Date). <u>Title</u>. Place of publication: Publisher.	Lim, S. (Ed.). (2000). <u>Asian-American literature: An anthology</u>. New York: McGraw-Hill.
Periodicals	**Example**
With an Author Author's Last Name, First & Second Initial. Date (Year, Month day). Article title. <u>Periodical Title, volume</u>, page range.	Hersh, S. M. (2004, May 10). Torture at Abu Ghraib. <u>New Yorker , 80</u>, 42-47.
With Multiple Authors [For listing the authors' names, follow the instructions above for 2-6 authors]. Date (year, month day). Article title. <u>Periodical Title, volume</u>, page range.	Nelson, D. R., Hammen, C., Brennan, P. A., & Ullman, J. B. (2003, October). The impact of maternal depression on adolescent adjustment: The role of expressed emotion. <u>Journal of Counseling and Clinical Psychology, 71</u>, 935-944.
Without an Author Article title. Date (year, month day). <u>Periodical Title, volume</u>, page range.	Vietnamese Americans: Lessons in American history. (2004, Spring). <u>Teaching Tolerance, 25</u>, 31-35.
Print Encyclopedias, Reference Works	**Example**
With an Author Author's Last Name, First & Second Initial. (Date). Article title. In <u>Encyclopedia title</u> (Vol., page range). Place of Publication: Publisher.	Rook, K. S. (2000). Loneliness. In A. E. Kazden (Ed.), <u>Encyclopedia of psychology</u> (Vol. 5, pp. 73-76). New York: Oxford University Press.
Without an Author Article Title. (Date). In <u>Encyclopedia title</u> (Vol., page range). Place of Publication: Publisher.	United Nations. (1993). In <u>Columbia encyclopedia</u> (5th ed., pp. 2826-2828). New York: Columbia University Press.

APA—Online Resources

Online Periodicals	Example
Article in Online Newspaper Author's Last Name, First & Second Initial. Date (year, month day). Article title. <u>Periodical title</u>. Retrieval statement with access date and URL	Pierre, R. E. (2004, May 11). In Ohio, Supreme Court considers right to procreate. <u>Washington Post</u>. Retrieved May 11, 2004, from http://www.washingtonpost.com
Article in Online Magazine, Journal Author's Last Name, First & Second Initial. Date. Article title. <u>Periodical title, volume</u>. Retrieval statement with access date and URL	Boutin, P. (2004, March). The case for staying off Mars. <u>Wired magazine</u>. Retrieved May 11, 2004, from http://www.wired.com/wired/archive/12.03/start.html?pg=14
Internet Sites	**Example**
With an Author Author's Last Name, First & Second Initials. (Date). Article or section title. In <u>Title of Internet site or Web page</u>. Retrieval statement with access date (month day, year) and URL that links directly to chapter or section	Gray, T. A. (2003, October 28). A Shakespeare timeline. In <u>Mr. William Shakespeare and the Internet</u>. Retrieved May 6, 2004, from http://shakespeare.palomar.edu/timeline/timeline. htm
Without an Author Article title. (Date). <u>Title of Internet site or Web page</u>. Retrieval statement with access date (month day, year) and URL that links directly to chapter or section	Black death, 1348. (2004, May 4) In <u>Eye witness to history</u>. Retrieved May 6, 2004, from http://www.eyewitnesstohistory.com/plague.htm
Online Encyclopedias, Reference Works	**Example**
With an Author Author's Last Name, First & Second Initial. (Date). Article title. In <u>Encyclopedia Title</u>. Retrieval statement with access date (month day, year) and URL that links directly to chapter or section if possible, or to home page	Katz, E. (2000). Margaret Sanger. In <u>American national biography online</u>. Retrieved May 6, 2004, from http://www.anb.org/articles/home.html
Without an Author Article title. (Date). In <u>Encyclopedia Title</u>. Retrieval statement with access date (month day, year) and URL that links directly to chapter or section if possible, or to home page	Landscape architecture. (2004). In <u>Encyclopedia Britannica</u>. Retrieved May 6, 2004, from Encyclopedia Britannica Premium Service: http://www.Britannica.com/eb/article?eu=48157
Subscription Service Databases	**Example**
Online Database Author's Last Name, First & Second Initial. (Date). Article title. <u>Periodical Title, volume</u>, page range. Retrieval statement with access date (month day, year) and Name of database.	Herzog, S. J. (1999, January). Wind energy: Power and policy. <u>Appraisal Journal, 67</u>, 24+. Retrieved May 7, 2004, from InfoTrac Expanded Academic ASAP database.
CD-ROM Author's Last Name, First & Second Initial. (Date). Article title. <u>Periodical Title, volume</u>, page range. Retrieval statement with access date (month day, year) and Name of database.	Dunn, S. (1999, September/October). King coal's weakening grip on power. <u>World Watch</u>, 10-19. Retrieved May 7, 2004, from SIRS Researcher database.
Non-Subscription Databases	**Example**
Organization Web site, with Author Author's Last Name, First & Second Initial. (Date). Article title. Retrieval statement with access date (day month, year), and Institution or Organization Name: URL	Ebadi, S. (2004, May 3). Human rights and economic development [Video]. Retrieved May 9, 2004, from World Bank Web site: http://worldbank.org
Organization Web site, without Author Article Title. Retrieval statement with access date (day month, year), and Institution or Organization Name: URL	List of member states. (2003, April 24). Retrieved May 9, 2004, from United Nations Web site: http://www.un.org/Overview/unmember. html

Index

A

American Psychological Association. See APA

APA, 5, 125–30; APA Publication Manual, 5, 131, 169, 176; guidelines, 169

C

capitalization, 10, 52, 58, 107, 144; article, chapter, book (APA), 170; examples (APA), 170; initial capitals, 108; magazine or newspaper (APA), 170; references (APA), 170; titles, 131; works cited (MLA), 154

CD-ROMs, 15, 19, 28, 164, 179

conclusions, 135–42; concluding sentences, 138; good conclusion attributes, 139; thesis statement, 138, 141

correction symbols, 149–51

D

databases, 15, 16, 17, 19, 20, 21, 28, 227; online information, 16–20; subscription, 21

dictionaries: britannica.com, 224

direct quotations, 9, 10, 80, 87, 92, 96, 101, 107–17, 107, 108, 109, 111, 144; end of the sentence (APA), 127; examples, 109; extended quotation (APA), 127; extended quotation (MLA), 122; follow-ups, 108, 113–16; introductory phrases, 91; lead-ins, 110; long quotations, 109; minor alterations, 109; parenthetical

documentation (APA), 125; parenthetical documentation (MLA), 119, 121

E

electronic resources, 15, 51, 160

ellipsis, 87, 108

encyclopedias-online, 18

F

focusing sentences, 135

follow-ups, 108, 113–16, 114, 115, 144

formatting, 146

formulating a thesis statement, 35–38

G

Getting Stupid, 65

Getting Stupid-annotated, 72

I

information: targeting, 61–64

Internet, 16, 21–23; choosing search words, 21; meta-search tools, 222–23; pitfalls, 23; search engines, 219–30; searching, 21; ten tips, 21

introductory paragraphs, 135–42; adding zip, 136; examples, 136; focusing sentences, 135; method of development (MOD), 136; thesis statement, 135

L

lead-ins, 62, 92, 108, 110, 111, 144; credentials, 112; examples, 108, 112; rules for use, 111

libraries, 15, 16, 20, 169, 224–25; databases, 20; public, 15, 20; university, 15, 20

M

media centers, 1, 15, 20, 169; audio/video resources, 15; CD-ROMs, 15; databases, 15; electronic resources, 15; print resources, 15; subscription databases, 21

meta-search tools, 222–23; dogpile.com, 223; ixquick.com, 223; mamma.com, 223; metacrawler.com, 223; profusion.com, 223

method of development. See MOD

MLA, 5, 51, 131, 160; MLA Handbook, 5, 12, 131, 154, 160; works cited, 120

MOD, 2, 39–42, 40, 136, 144, 187

model research papers: Jason Rosensweig, 196; Jeffrey Dickinson, 211; Portia Cornell, 188; Simon Chin, 203

Modern Language Association. See MLA

N

netmyth, 23

note cards, 2, 3, 10, 47, 61, 63, 79, 80, 81, 85, 88, 91, 92, 93, 147, 153; examples, 84, 86, 88, 94; subheadings, 86; topic headings, 85, 86; topic outlines, 47; word-for-word, 87

note taking, 39, 40, 85–90, 85; avoiding plagiarism, 87; direct quotations, 80, 87; ellipsis, 87; examples, 63,

84; how-to steps, 85; retention of errors, 109

O

online encyclopedias, 18

online resources, 16–20

P

paraphrasing, 3, 10, 80, 87, 91, 92, 101–3, 102, 110, 147; careless, 91; example, 10

parenthetical documentation, 11, 92, 103, 108; MLA, 119–24, 120, 121

periodicals: online resources, 16–17

plagiarism, 7–12, 7, 8, 10, 23, 85, 87, 119, 125, 147; avoiding, 8, 11; checking citations, 11; cite as you write, 11; consequences, 8; direct quotations, 9; examples, 7; Internet resources, 12; paraphrasing, 9; rules, 8; self-plagiarism, 11

primary sources, 185, 186; direct quotations, 107

proofreading. *See* revising

punctuation, 144; direct quotations, 107; MLA, 153

Q

quotation marks, 9, 107; internet searching, 219

quotations, 80; poor use of, 91

R

radio or television, 165, 180

references (APA), 3, 4, 11, 58, 126, 147, 169–81, 169; abstract, 173; audio recording, 176; audio visual media, 175; book chapter or article, 174; books, 173; brochure, 174; capitalization, 170; CD-

ROM programs, 179; citation examples, 235, 236; dictionaries, 174; electronic resources, 176; e-mail, 180; encyclopedias, 174; examples, 170–81, 218; form and accuracy, 11; format, 169; government agency, 174; journal article, 172; magazine article, 172; monograph, 173; music recording, 176; newsletter, 172; newspaper article, 172; online book, 178; online database, 176, 177; online document, 176; online interview, 180; online journal, 178; online magazine article, 179; online newspaper article, 178; online painting, sculpture, or photograph, 180; online posting, 181; online project, 176; online review, 178; other electronic sources, 180; periodicals, 172; proceedings, 175; punctuation, 169; quotation marks, 169; radio, 180; references page format, 169; review, 175; sample reference page, 171; source cards, 169; technical reports, 174; television, 175, 180; unpublished paper, 175

references (MLA). See works cited (MLA); references page format, 170

relevant material, 61–83; examples, 79–82; sample, 84

resources: online content services, 18–20; online encyclopedias, 18; online periodicals, 16–17

revising, 3, 143–52; capitalization, 144; checklist, 146; correction symbols, 143, 149–51; descriptive text, 144; expository writing rules, 144; grammar usage, 144;

punctuation, 144; sentence structure, 143; spelling, 145; strong verbs, 143; transition words, 144; word choice, 143

rough draft, 3, 80, 91–99; follow-ups, 93; necktie effect, 91; process example, 94; step-by-step procedure, 91–93

S

search engines, 21, 219–30, 221, 223; Boolean operators (AND, OR, and NOT), 220; case sensitivity, 219; Internet libraries, 227; literature, arts, humanities, 227; news and current events, 226; NewsIndex, 226; NewsLink, 226; NewsTrawler, 226; proximity operator (NEAR), 220; quotation marks, 219; science, 229; search tool terminology, 219; search tools, 219–20, 222; social science, 229

secondary sources, 185–86, 186; direct quotation, 107

source cards (APA), 56–60, 169; adding comments to, 58; articles, 56; books, 56, 58; capitalization, 58; corrections, 58; examples, 60; quotation marks, 58; recording information on, 57; required information, 57; samples, 56, 60

source cards (MLA), 50–52, 80; articles, 50; books, 50, 52; capitalization, 52; correct form, 51; correcting, 52; entries on, 51; examples, 50

sources: primary, 185; secondary, 185

subject directories, 224–25; britannica.com, 224; infomine.ucr.edu, 224; internet scout project, 224; librarians index, 225;

looksmart.com, 225; open directory project, 225

summarizing, 3, 87, 92, 103–5

supporting topics, 39, 79; examples, 39

T

thesis statements, 2, 29, 31, 35–38, 35, 40, 48, 79, 88, 92, 135, 136, 137, 141, 144, 187; conclusions, 138; examples, 35–37; note taking, 85; revising, 91; supporting, 39–42; supporting topics, 39

titles, 3; capitalization, 131; quotation marks, 132, 133; using correctly, 131–34

topic headings, 2, 81; examples, 85; note taking, 85

topic outlines, 2, 3, 45–48, 91; example, 46–47; major topics, 46–47; position paper, 184; preliminary, 46; research paper, 183

topic selection, 27–30; attributes for excellence, 27; brainstorming, 28; narrowing the topic, 27, 31–33; preliminary work, 28; questions to ask, 29

topics, 81; major topics, 3; subtopics, 3

W

web site evaluation form, 230, 231–32

works cited (APA). See references

works cited (MLA), 3, 4, 11, 51, 52, 119, 120, 122, 147, 153–68; anthology, 156; audio, 159; books, 120, 156; capitalization, 154; CD-ROMs, 164; correct form, 51; editorial, 158; electronic resources, 160; e-mail, 167; examples, 155–67, 195, 202, 210, 233, 234; form and accuracy, 11; format for works cited page, 154; government publication, 157; interview, 159, 160; letter, 159; letter to the editor, 159; magazine article, 158; map, 160, 166; multivolume work, 158; musical composition, 159; newspaper, 158; note cards, 153; online audio, 166; online book, 162; online database, 161; online document, 161; online government publication, 163; online interview, 166; online map, 166; online painting, sculpture, or photograph, 166; online periodicals, 163; online posting, 167; online project, 161; online video, 166; other electronic sources, 165; other sources, 159; painting or photograph, 166; pamphlet, 157; performance, 159; periodicals, 158; punctuation, 153; radio, 159; recording, 159; reference work, 157; review, 159; sample works cited page, 155; scholarly journal, 158; source cards, 153; speech, 160; television, 159; video, 159; work of art, 159

World Wide Web, 5, 21, 22